Phillips Brooks

Sermons Preached in English Churches

Phillips Brooks

Sermons Preached in English Churches

ISBN/EAN: 9783337087869

Printed in Europe, USA, Canada, Australia, Japan

Cover: Foto ©Lupo / pixelio.de

More available books at **www.hansebooks.com**

SERMONS

Preached in English Churches

BY THE

REV. PHILLIPS BROOKS

RECTOR OF TRINITY CHURCH, BOSTON, MASSACHUSETTS

London
MACMILLAN AND CO.
1885

Printed by R. & R. CLARK, *Edinburgh.*

TO

MANY FRIENDS IN ENGLAND

IN REMEMBRANCE OF THEIR CORDIAL WELCOME

I INSCRIBE THESE SERMONS

CONTENTS.

		PAGE
I.	THE PATTERN IN THE MOUNT	1

"See that thou make all things according to the pattern shewed to thee in the mount."—HEBREWS viii. 5.

II. THE MIND'S LOVE FOR GOD 22

"Jesus said unto him, Thou shalt love the Lord thy God . . . with all thy mind."—MATTHEW xxii. 37.

III. THE FIRE AND THE CALF 43

"So they gave it me: then I cast it into the fire and there came out this calf."—EXODUS xxxii. 24.

IV. MAN'S WONDER AND GOD'S KNOWLEDGE . 65

"Thus saith the Lord of hosts: If it be marvellous in the eyes of the remnant of this people in these days, should it also be marvellous in mine eyes? saith the Lord of hosts."—ZECHARIAH viii. 6.

V. IN THE LIGHT OF GOD 89

"In thy light we shall see light."—PSALM xxxvi. 9.

VI. THE SUFFICIENT GRACE OF GOD . . . 112

"And he said, My grace is sufficient for thee."—2 CORINTHIANS xii. 9.

VII. THE CHRISTIAN CITY 134

"And there was great joy in that city."—ACTS viii. 8.

		PAGE
VIII.	THE GREATNESS OF FAITH	157

"Then Jesus answered and said unto her, O woman, great is thy faith: be it unto thee even as thou wilt."—MATTHEW xv. 28.

IX.	"WHY COULD NOT WE CAST HIM OUT?"	179

"Then came the disciples to Jesus apart, and said, Why could not we cast him out?"—MATTHEW xvii. 9.

X.	NATURE AND CIRCUMSTANCES	200

"Verily I say unto you, Among them that are born of women there hath not risen a greater than John the Baptist: notwithstanding he that is least in the kingdom of heaven is greater than he."—MATTHEW xi. 11.

XI.	THE WILLING SURRENDER	221

"Thinkest thou that I cannot now pray to my Father, and he shall presently give me more than twelve legions of angels? But how then shall the scriptures be fulfilled, that thus it must be?"—MATTHEW xxvi. 53.

XII.	GAMALIEL	243

"Gamaliel, a doctor of the law, had in reputation among all the people."—ACTS v. 34.

XIII.	THE GIFT AND ITS RETURN	265

"For with what measure ye mete, it shall be measured to you again.'—MATTHEW vii. 2.

XIV.	"YOUR JOY NO MAN TAKETH FROM YOU"	288

"And your joy no man taketh from you."—JOHN xvi. 22.

I.

THE PATTERN IN THE MOUNT.[1]

"See that thou make all things according to the pattern shewed to thee in the mount."—HEBREWS viii. 5.

THE elements which make a perfect work are two—a perfect workman, and a perfect pattern. A perfect workman must have perfect faithfulness and perfect skill; and so, to make any accomplishment entirely complete, faithfulness and skill must join in the fulfilment of the perfect plan. It is very much like the casting of some great work in metal. There is skill in the mixing of the elements. Faithfulness is like the pervading heat which keeps the whole mass fluid. But the plan or pattern of the work is like the mould into which the well-mixed and molten metal must be poured, that it may get form and value, and not remain a merely shapeless mass.

There are, then, two great reasons why men's

[1] Preached at St. Botolph's Church, Boston, Lincolnshire, Sunday morning, 2d July 1882; and at the Chapel Royal, Savoy, London, Sunday morning, 20th May 1883.

works are failures: one is the lack of the personal qualities of faithfulness and skill in the worker; the other is the absence of a pattern, or the presence of a wrong pattern, in which the faithfulness and skill take shape. The first kind of failure is common enough. Plenty of people there are who, with most perfect plans of life, are so unfaithful or unskilful that their lives come to nothing. But the second kind of failure also is abundant. The world is full of men who, with great faithfulness and skill are doing little, because the plan, the standard, the pattern of their life is weak or wrong. To them, and of them, let me speak to-day, using for my text these words out of the old Epistle to the Hebrews: "See that thou make all things according to the pattern shewed to thee in the mount."

The warning had been given to Moses when he was about to make the Tabernacle. The leader of the Jews was full of faithfulness, and all the skill of all the people was at his command. He could make what he would; but never in all the world before had there been such a tabernacle as he was now to build. There was no precedent or accepted rule. And so we read in Exodus that God called him up into a high mountain, and there, in some mysterious way, He gave His servant a description of the Tabernacle which He wanted him to build. He showed it to him in elaborate detail, and when, upon the seventh day, Moses came down from Mount Sinai, the unbuilt Tabernacle was already in existence in his mind, as it had been already before in existence in the mind of God. Not yet had it any material existence; but its idea was there. It was not visible or tangible. The gold, the silver, and the brass, the blue and purple and scarlet, the fine linen and goats' hair, the rams' skins dyed red, the brilliant lamps and carved cherubs shone as yet in no earthly sunshine; the fragrance of the spices floated on no earthly air; the curtains waved in no terrestrial breezes; the stakes which held the structure had been driven in no field of our common ground; it was not yet in being as a material fact, a bright, strange apparition, such as by and by moved with the host of the Israelites and filled the tribes of their enemies with wonder. But yet, in a true sense, it was—it had existence, when God had opened the chamber of His will in which the idea of the unbuilt Tabernacle already stood complete, and showed it to His servant. All that afterwards took place, all the slow building of the Tabernacle by the offerings of the people, was but the transference from the region of ideas to the region of realities of that which existed already in the mind of God.

We have only to enlarge the conception which is in this story and to make it general, and we come at once to one of the loftiest and most inspiring thoughts of human life. As the old Tabernacle, before it was built, existed in the mind of God, so all the unborn things of life, the things which are to make the future, are already living in their perfect ideas in Him, and when the future comes, its task will be to match those divine ideas with their material realities, to translate into the visible and tangible shapes of terrestrial life the facts which already have existence in the perfect mind. Surely in the very statement of such a thought of life there is something which ennobles and dignifies our living. It takes something of this dreadful extemporaneousness and superficialness and incoherence out of our life. The things which come to pass here in the world are not mere volunteer efforts of man's enterprise, not self-contained ventures which are responsible to nothing and to no one but themselves. For each of them there is an idea present already in the thought of God, a pattern of what each in its purest perfection is capable of being. Out of the desire to realise that idea must come the highest inspiration. In the degree to which it has realised that idea must be the standard of judgment of every work of man. To-day begins a baby's life.

A child is born into the world this Sunday morning. What shall we say about that child's unlived life? No man can tell what it will be. Its lessons are unlearned, its tasks untried, its discoveries unmade, its loves unloved, its growth entirely ungrown, as the little new-born problem lies unsolved on this the first day of its life. Is that all? Is there nowhere in the universe any picture of what that child's life ought to be, and may be? Surely there is. If God is that child's Father, then in the Father's mind, in God's mind, there must surely be a picture of what that child with his peculiar faculties and nature may become in the completeness of his life. Years hence, when that baby of to-day has grown to be the man of forty, the real question of his life will be, what? Not the questions which his fellow-citizens of that remote day will be asking, What reputation has he won? What money has he earned? Not even, What learning has he gained? But, How far has he been able to translate into the visible and tangible realities of a life that idea which was in God's mind on that day in the old year when he was born? How does the tabernacle which he has built correspond with the pattern which is in the mount? Ah, somewhere in the universe of God, dear friends—if not among our brethren beside us, if not by our own hearts—

somewhere in the universe, that question is being asked to-day of every one of us who has grown up and left his youth behind him. Moses may, if he will, go on and build a tabernacle to suit himself, and as its self-willed architecture rises, the people may gather around it and call it wonderful, and praise the builder's genius, but God's eye is judging it all the time simply by one standard, simply by its conformity or non-conformity to the pattern which, long before the hewing of the first beam or the weaving of the first curtain, existed in the mount.

All this is true not merely of a whole life as a whole, but of each single act or enterprise of life. We have not thought richly or deeply enough about any undertaking unless we have thought of it as an attempt to put into the form of action that which already has existence in the idea of God. You start upon your profession, and your professional career in its perfect conception shines already in God's sight. Already before Him there is the picture of the good physician, the broad-minded merchant, the fair-minded lawyer, the heroic minister, which you may be. You set yourself down to some hard struggle with temptation, and already in the fields of God's knowledge you are walking as possible victor, clothed in white and with the crown of victory upon your head. You build your house, and found your home. It is an attempt to realise the picture of purity, domestic peace, mutual inspiration and mutual comfort, which God sees already. Your friendship which begins to shape itself to-day out of your intercourse with your companion has its pattern in the vast treasury of God's conceptions of what man, with perfect truthfulness and perfect devotion, may be to his brother man. It is not vulgar fate and destiny; it is not a mere settlement beforehand by God's foreknowledge of what each man must be and do, so that he cannot escape. The man's will is still free. The man may falsify God's picture of him, he certainly will fall short of it; but it is the essential truth of the Father comprehending all his children's lives within His own, the infinite nature containing the finite natures in itself and holding in itself their standard.

The distinction between ideas and forms is one which all men need to know, which many men so often seem to miss. The idea takes shape in the form, the form expresses the idea. The form, without the idea behind it, is thin and hard. The form, continually conscious of its idea, becomes rich, deep, and elastic. He who once gets the sight into that world of ideas which lies unseen behind the world of forms never can lose sight of it again, never can be content with any act of his until he has carried it into that world and matched it with its idea. To the man who is trying to do just or generous things, but who is perpetually conscious of how imperfect is the justice or the generosity of the things he does, it is a constant incentive and comfort to be sure that somewhere, in God, there is the perfect type and pattern of the thing of which he fails. That certainty at once preserves the loftiness of his standard and saves him from despair. This is the power of ideality, of the unfailing sight of the perfect ideas behind the imperfect form of things.

If all that I have said be true, then it would seem as if there ought to be in the world three kinds of men—the men of forms; the men of limited ideals, or of ideals which are not the highest; and the men of unlimited ideals, or the highest ideals, which are the ideals of God. And three such kinds of men there are, very distinct and easy of discovery. First, there are the men of forms, the men who, in all their self-questionings about what they ought to do, and in all their judgments about what they have done, never get beyond the purely formal standards which proceed either from the necessity of their conditions or from the accepted precedents of other people. They never get into the regions of ideas at all.

How many such men there are! To them the question of their business life never comes up so high as to mean, "What is the best and loftiest way in which it is possible for this business of mine to be done?" It never gets higher than to mean, "How can I best support myself by my business?" or else, "What are the rules and ways of business which are most accepted in the business world?" To such men the question of religion never becomes: "What are the intrinsic and eternal relations between the Father God and man the child?" but only, "By what religious observances can a man get into heaven?" or else, "What is the most current religion of my fellow-men?" There is no unseen type of things after the pattern of which the seen deed must be shaped. Every deed is single and arbitrary and special, a thing done and to be judged, not by its conformity to some eternal standard of what such a deed ought to be, but simply by its fitness to produce results. Such a man judges a deed like a hatchet, solely by whether it will split wood. The deed no more than the hatchet has any true character, any conformity to or departure from an essential and eternal type. Of course no visions haunt a man like that. He dreams no dreams of finer purity and loftiness which might have given a more subtle and divine success to acts of his which the world calls successful. He lives in a low self-content, and knows no pain or disappointment at his actions unless his act fails of its visible result, or unless other men condemn the method in which he happens to have acted.

It would be sad, indeed, to think that there is any man here to-day who has not at least sometimes in his life got a glimpse into a richer and fuller and more interesting sort of life than this. There is a second sort of man who does distinctly ask himself whether his deed is what it ought to be. He is not satisfied with asking whether it works its visible result or not, whether other men praise it or not. There is another question still, Does it conform to what he knew before he undertook it that it ought to be? If it does not, however it may seem successful, however men may praise it, the doer of the deed turns off from it in discontent. If it does, no matter how it seems to fail, no matter how men blame it, he thanks God for it and is glad. Here is a true idealism; here is a man with an unseen pattern and standard for his work. He lives a loftier, and likewise a more unquiet life. He goes his way with his vision before his eyes. "I know something of what this piece of work ought to have been," he says, "therefore I cannot be satisfied with it as it is." What is the defect of such an idealism as that? It is, that as yet the idea comes only from the man's own self. Therefore, although it lies farther back than the mere form, it does not lie entirely at the back of everything. It is not final; it shares the incompleteness of the man from whom it springs. It may be born of prejudice and selfishness. It is the source very often of bigotry and uncharitableness and superstition. These are not seldom the fruits of narrow ideality. The man of no ideas is not a bigot. The man of largest ideas has outgrown bigotry. It is the man who asks for principles, the man who seeks to conform his life to some conception of what life ought to be, but who seeks his pattern no higher and no deeper than his own convictions, it is he who stands in danger of, and very often falls into narrowness and pride and the insolent, uncharitable demand that all men shall shape their lives in the same form as his.

Therefore it is that something more is needed, and that only the third man's life is wholly satisfactory. I said that he not merely looked for an idea to which he wanted to conform his life, but he looked for that idea in God. Literally and truly he believes that the life he is to live, the act he is to do, lies now, a true reality, already existent and present, in the mind of God; and his object, his privilege, is not simply to see how he can live his life in the way which will look best or produce the most brilliant visible result, not simply to see how he can best carry out his own personal idea of what is highest and best, but how he can most truly reproduce on earth that image of this special life or action which is in the perfect mind. This is the way in which he is to make all things according to the pattern which is in the mount.

Does it sound at first as if there were something almost slavish in such a thought as that? He who thinks so has not begun to apprehend the essential belonging together of the life of God and the life of every man. For man to accept the pattern of his living absolutely from any other being besides God in all the universe would be for him to sacrifice his self and to lose his originality. But for man to find and simply reproduce the picture of his life which is in God is for him not to sacrifice but to find his self. For the man is in God. The ideal, the possible perfection of everything that he can do or be, is there in God; and to be original for any man is not to start aside with headlong recklessness and do what neither brother-man, nor God dreamed of our doing; but it is to do with filial loyalty the act which, because God is God, a being such as we are ought to do under the circumstances, in the conditions in which we stand. Because no other being ever was or ever will be just the same as you, and because precisely the same conditions never before have been and never will be grouped about any other mortal life as are grouped around yours, therefore for you to do and be what you, with your own nature in your own circumstances, ought in the judgment of the perfect mind to do and be, that is originality for you.

What quiet independence, what healthy humility, what confident hope there must be in this man who thus goes up to God to get the pattern of his living. To-morrow morning to that man there comes a great overwhelming sorrow. Bereavement breaks open his house's guarded door, and the unbroken circle is shattered at what seemed its dearest and safest spot. The man looks about and questions himself—What shall he do, what shall he be in this new terrible life, terrible not least because of its awful newness, which has burst upon him? Where shall he find the pattern for his new necessity? Of course he may look about and copy the forms with which the world at large greets and denotes its sorrow, the decent dreadful conventionalities of grief. He may alter his dress and moderate his walk and tone, and even hide himself from sight, and so give all his pain its proper form. That does not satisfy him. The world acknowledges that he has borne his grief most properly, but he is not satisfied. Then, behind all that, he may reason it over with himself, think out what death means, make his philosophy, decide how a man ought to behave in the terrible shipwreck of his hopes. That is a better thing by all means than the other. But this man does something more. The pattern of his new life is not in the world. It is not in himself. It is in God. He goes up to find it. There is, lying in God's mind, an image of him, this very man, with this very peculiar nature of his, of him bearing this particular sorrow, and trained by it into a peculiar strength, which can belong to no other man in all the world. That image is a reality in God's soul before it becomes a visible thing in the man's soul living on the earth. To get up, then, into God, and find that image of his grieved and sorrowing life, and then come back and shape his life after it patiently and cheerfully, that is the struggle of the Christian idealist in his sorrow, of the man who tries to make all things according to the pattern which is in the mount. Can we not see what quiet independence, what healthy humility, what confident hope there must be in that man's struggle to live out through his sorrow the new life which his sorrow has made possible?

But now it is quite time for us to ask another

question. Suppose that all which we have said is true; suppose that there is such a pattern of the truest life, and of each truest act of every man lying in God's mind, how shall the man know what that pattern is? We can see into what a mockery our whole truth might be misread. "Yes," one might say, "God has in Himself the true idea of you, but what of that? How will that help you? You cannot go up into His mind to find it there. You must go on still blundering and guessing, only trembling to know that at the last you will be judged by a standard of which you could never get a sight while you were working at your life. Look up, poor soul, out of the valley and know that on the top of yonder shining mountain lies folded safe the secret of your life, the oracle which would, if you could read it, solve all your mysteries and tell you just exactly how you ought to live. Look up out of the valley and know that it is there; and then turn back again into the valley, for in the valley is the home where you must live, and you can never read the oracle which you know is there upon the mountain-top." What mockery could there be like that? How must the poor man bend his head like a beast and go plodding on, refusing to look at, trying to forget, the mountain where his secret lay, and where he must not climb! Is that the fate of man who knows that in God lies the image and the pattern of his life? It might seem to be, it has very often seemed to be, but it can never really be to any one who really knows and believes in the Incarnation, the life of the God-Man among men. Do you not see? Is not Christ the mountain up into which the believer goes, and in which he finds the divine idea of himself. As a mountain seems to be the meeting-place of earth and heaven, the place where the bending skies meet the aspiring planet, the place where the sunshine and the cloud keep closest company with the granite and the grass: so Christ is the meeting-place of divinity and humanity; He is at once the condescension of divinity and the exaltation of humanity; and man wanting to know God's idea of man, any man wanting to know God's idea of him, must go up into Christ, and he will find it there.

I would not have that sound to you fanciful and vague, for I am sure that there is in that statement the most sure and practical of truths. It was so in the old days of the visible incarnation. See how, when Jesus walked on earth, the men and women who were with Him there were always climbing up into the mountain of His life, and seeing there what God's idea of their lives was. A young man, puzzled with matching commandments, weary of wondering which little corner of duty he should make his own, came up to Christ, came up into Christ, and asked, " Lord, which is the great commandment ? " and instantly, as Christ looked at him and answered him, the man saw a new vision of himself, a vision of a life filled with a passionate love of the Holy One, and so he went back determined not to rest until he had attained all holiness. If he came down from Christ a larger man, giving his whole life thenceforth to the attainment of the love of God, and letting all duty do itself out of the abundance of that love, that was the way in which he did all things according to the pattern which had been shewed to him on the mount. Into that mountain of the Lord went up John Boanerges, to see God's idea of him as the man of love ; and fickle-hearted Peter, to see God's idea of him as the steadfast rock ; and trembling Mary Magdalene, to know herself beloved and forgiven. Nay, up that mountain went even Judas Iscariot, far enough to catch sight of God's Judas, of the man resisting temptation and loyally faithful to his Lord. Up that mountain went Pontius Pilate, and for a moment we can see flash before his eyes the ideal of himself, the true Roman, the true man, God's Pilate, brave and honest, unscared by shouting Jews or frowning Cæsar, standing by his convictions and protecting his helpless prisoner against His brutal enemies. Every man who came to Jesus saw in Him the image of his own true self, the thing that he might be and ought to be. Hundreds of them were not ready for the sight, and turned and went their way, to be not what they might be, nor what they ought to be, but what they basely chose to be. But none the less the pattern had been shewed to them in the mount.

And so it has been ever since. All kinds of men have found their ideals in Jesus. Entering into Him, the timid soul has seen a vision of itself all clothed in bravery, and known in an instant that to be brave and not to be cowardly was its proper life. The missionary toiling in the savage island, and thinking his whole life a failure, has gone apart some night into his hut and climbed up into Christ, and seen with perfect sureness, though with most complete amazement, that God counted his life a great success, and so has gone out once more singing to his glorious work. Martyrs on the night before their agony; reformers hesitating at their tasks; scholars wondering whether the long self-denial would be worth their while; fathers and mothers, teachers and preachers whose work had grown monotonous and wearisome, all of these going to Christ have found themselves in Him, have seen the nobleness and privilege of their hard lives, and have come out from their communion with Him to live their lives as they had seen those lives in Him, glorious with the perpetual sense of the privilege of duty, and worthy of the best and most faithful work which they could give.

Cannot you go to Christ to-day and find the idea of yourself in Him. It is certainly there. In Christ's thought at this moment there is a picture of you which is perfectly distinct and separate and clear. It is not a vague blurred picture of a good man with all the special colours washed away, with nothing to distinguish it from any other good man in the town. It is a picture of you. It is you with your own temptations conquered, and your own type of goodness, different from any other man's in all the world, in all the ages, perfectly attained. If you give up your life to serving and loving Christ, one of the blessings of your consecration of yourself to Him, will be, that in Him there will open to you this pattern of yourself. You will see your possible self as He sees it, and then life will have but one purpose and wish for you, which will be that you may realise that idea of yourself which you have seen in Him.

This, then, is the great truth of Christ. The treasury of life, your life and mine, the life of every man and every woman, however different they are from one another, they are all in Him. In Him there is the perfectness of every occupation: the perfect trading, the perfect housekeeping, the perfect handicraft, the perfect school teaching, they are all in Him. In Him lay the completeness of that incomplete act which you did yesterday. In Him lay the possible holiness of that which you made actual sin. In Him lies the absolute purity and loftiness of that worship which we this morning have stained so with impurity and baseness. To go to Him and get the perfect idea of life, and of every action of life, and then to go forth, and by His strength fulfil it, that is the New Testament conception of a strong successful life. How simple and how glorious it is!

We are like Moses, then,—only our privilege is so much more than his. We are like a Moses who at any moment, whenever the building of the tabernacle flagged and hesitated, was able to turn and go up into the mountain and look once more the pattern in the face, and come down strong, ambitious for the best, and full of hope. So any moment we may turn from the poor reality to the great ideal of our own lives, which is in Christ, with one earnest question, "Lord, what wouldst Thou have me to be?" We may pierce through the clouds and reach the summit, and there, seeing His vision of our possibilities, be freed at once from our brethren's tyranny, and from our own content and sluggishness, and set to work with all our might to fulfil God's image of our lives, to be all that He has shown us that it is possible for us to be, to make all things in these valley lives of ours after the pattern shewed to us in the mount.

II.

THE MIND'S LOVE FOR GOD.[1]

"Jesus said unto him, Thou shalt love the Lord thy God . . . with all thy mind."—MATTHEW xxii. 37.

THIS is only part of a verse. It is a fragment of the injunction in which Christ laid down to His disciples the whole range and compass of the Christian life. In words which must have seemed to each of them, according to his character and mood, either the imposition of a duty or the offer of a privilege which was large enough to cover and fill all their lives, their Lord had said to them, " Thou shalt love the Lord thy God with all thy heart, and with all thy soul, and with all thy mind. This is the first and great commandment. And the second is like unto it, Thou shalt love thy neighbour as thyself." The two great commandments make one duty. Completely carried out in all their parts, they would make life a

[1] Preached at St. Mark's Church, Upper Hamilton Terrace, London, Sunday morning, 13th May 1883.

strong and perfect unit. But, as we study them, it is possible to take their unity apart and fix our thoughts upon a single one of the elements of which it is composed. This is what I want to do this morning; for there is one part of the great comprehensive statement of duty which, often as we repeat it, I think that many of us seldom pause to consider and have seldom consciously and conscientiously tried to work out into life. It is that in which Jesus says, "Thou shalt love the Lord thy God with all thy mind." Far more familiar is the thought which is included in the other words, "Thou shalt love God with all thy heart and soul." The affections of the emotional nature we think of very often. That the soul, which is the very seat of admiring wonder and of spiritual sympathy, should glow and burn at the sight of the excellence and love of God, we all see and feel how natural that is. But that the mind must love, that the intellectual nature also has its affections which it must give to God; this, perhaps, seems to us more strange; certainly it is less familiar.

But yet if it is true, we surely want to understand it. If there is one part of our nature which we have been in the habit of thinking either had nothing to do with our religion or else could only deal with our religion in the coldest and hardest way, but which, indeed, is capable of burning with its own peculiar fire, surely it will be worth our while to study it as carefully as we can. This is why I ask you to think with me this morning, about the Christian loving God with all his mind.

In the first place, then, we want to assure ourselves in general that there is such a power as intellectual affection, and that no man completely and worthily loves any noble thing or person unless he loves it with his mind as well as with his heart and soul. That will not, I think, be very hard to see. Take, for instance, your love for some beautiful scene of nature. There is somewhere upon the earth a lordly landscape which you love. When you are absent from it, you remember it with delight and longing. When you step into the sight of it after long absence, your heart thrills and leaps. While you sit quietly gazing day after day upon it, your whole nature rests in peace and satisfaction. Now, what is it in you that loves that loveliness? Love I take to be the delighted perception of the excellence of things. With what do you delightedly perceive how excellent is all that makes up that landscape's beauty, the bending sky, the rolling hill, the sparkling lake, the waving harvest, and the brooding mist? First of all, no doubt, with your senses. It is the seeing eye, the hearing ear, the sense of feeling which in the glowing cheek is soothed or made to tingle, the sense of smell which catches sweet odours from the garden or the hayfield,—it is these that love the landscape first; you love it first with all your senses. But next to that what comes? Suppose that the bright scene is radiant with associations, suppose that by that river you have walked with your most helpful friend; upon that lake you have floated and frolicked when you were a boy; across that field you have guided the staggering plough; over that hill you have climbed in days when life was all sunshine and breeze. That part of you which is capable of delightedly perceiving these associations as they shine up to you from the glowing scenery, perceives them with delight and takes the landscape into its affection. You love the scene with all your heart. But yet again, suppose a deeper faculty in you perceives the hand of God in all this wondrous beauty; suppose a glad and earnest gratitude springs up in you and goes to meet the meadow and the sky; suppose that all seems to tell to some deep listening instinct in you that it was all made for you, and made by one who loved you; suppose that it all stands as a rich symbol of yet richer spiritual benefits of which you are aware; what then? Does not another part of you spring up and pour out its affection, your power of reverence and gratefulness ; and so you love the landscape then with all your soul. Or yet again, if the whole scene appears to tempt you with invitations to work : the field calling on you to till it, and the river to bridge it, and the hill to set free the preciousness of gold or silver with which its heart is full and heavy; to that too you respond with your power of working ; and then you love the scene with all your will, or all your strength.

And now, suppose that, beyond all these, another spirit comes out from the landscape to claim another yet unclaimed part of you ; suppose that unsolved problems start out from the earth and from the sky. Glimpses of relationships between things and of qualities in things flit before you, just letting you see enough of them to set your curiosity all astir. The scene which cried before, " Come, admire me," or " Come, work on me," now cries, " Come, study me." What hangs the stars in their places and swings them on their way ; how the earth builds the stately tree out of the petty seed ; how the river feeds the cornfield ; where lie the metals in the mountains—these, and a hundred other questions, leap out from the picture before you and, pressing in, past your senses and your emotions and your practical powers, will not rest till they have found out your intelligence. They appeal to the mind, and the mind responds to them; not coldly, as if it had nothing to do but just to find and register their answers, but enthusiastically, perceiving with delight the excellence of the truths at which they point, recognising its appropriate task in their solution, and so loving the nature out of which they spring in its distinctive way.

Is not this clear? Is it not manifestly true that, besides the love of the senses, and the love of the heart, and the love of the soul, and the love of the strength, there is also a love of the mind, without whose entrance into the completeness of the loving man's relation to the object of his love his love is not complete? Think of the patriot's love for his land. Is it complete until the great ideas which lie at the basis of the country's life have appealed to the patriot's intellect, and his mind has enthusiastically recognised their truth and majesty? Is your greatest friend contented with your love before you have come to love him with all your mind? Will any fondness for his person, or association with his habits, or gratitude for his kindness, make up for the absence of intellectual sympathy, for a failure of your understanding to grasp the truths by which he lives? Everywhere we find our assurances that the mind has its affections and enthusiasms, that the intellect is no cold-hearted monster who only thinks and judges, but that it glows with love, not merely perceiving, but delighted to perceive, the beauty of the things with which it has to do.

It would be strange indeed if it were not so; strange indeed if the noblest part of us were incapable of the noblest action; strange indeed if, while our senses could thrill and our hearts leap with affection, the mind must go its way in pure indifference, making its great discoveries with no emotion for the truths which it discovered, and for the men in whom those truths were uttered. But it is not so. The intellect can love. The being who has intellect does not love perfectly unless his intellect takes part in his loving. We know that God loves man. The first article of all our faith in Him, next to His existence, is that He is no cold passive observer or manager of what goes on upon the earth, but that He loves the world and man in whom the deepest interest of the world resides. But can we think about God's love and not feel ever present as an element in it the working of the infinite mind as well as of the perfect heart? There is moral approbation, there is the father's tenderness, there is delight in the beauty of a good character. But the love on which we rest, and from which our most mighty inspirations come, is surely not complete until there also is in it the delight of the perfect intellect in the fitness of things, and joy in the adaptation of part to part, in the perfect sight of all the absolute harmony of laws and forces of which the little stray glimpses which we catch give the world a new sort of dearness in our eyes, and make us glow with enthusiasm as we, with our small judgments, speak God's words after Him and call it Good.

I know that I appear, as I speak thus, to separate into parts that which does really work as one unit. A being who completely loves something which is completely worthy of his love does not analyse himself with any such analysis as this which we have made. His affection is the affection of the one whole man. But when we force ourselves to analyse, I am sure we come to this, that the mind has its true distinctive power of affection, and that there is not a perfectness of love until that giant of the nature is present glowing with delight in truth.

No doubt men's minds differ from one another exceedingly in their capacity of affection. As we enter into the society of the great masters of human thought, it is a difference which we feel at once. Some great thinkers seem to deal with the things of which they think in passionless calmness. It seems as if they flung the truths they find abroad and cared no more for them, as the machine flings out the nails it makes. They seem to be almost like machinery which you can set at work on any material. But always there is another class of students and thinkers whose whole intellectual action is alive and warm. They love the truth they deal with. About such men there always is a charm peculiar to themselves. They evidently have a joy in their own work, and they make other people share their joy. We know such men at once. We are certain that the minds of the great theologians, from Paul to Maurice, loved their truths. We are sure that Shakespeare's intellect had an affection for its wonderful creations. The highest glory of the great students of natural science to-day is in the glowing love of which their minds are full for Nature and her truths. It is the necessity of any really creative genius. It is the soul of any true artistic work. Without it the most massive structures of human thought are as dead and heavy as the pyramids. With it the slightest product of man's mind springs into life, and, however slight it be, compels and fascinates attention.

I am sure that there is no wise and thoughtful teacher of young people whose whole experience has not borne witness often to what I am saying, that the mind has a power of directly loving truth which must be awakened before the learner is really able to do his best work. You tell your scholar that he must study because his parents wish it, because he ought to be equal to his fellow-scholars, because he will be poor and dishonoured if he is ignorant. These motives are good, but they are only the kindling under the fire. Not until an enthusiasm of your scholar's own intellect begins and he loves the books you offer him with his mind, because of the way they lay hold of his power of knowing them; not until then has the wood really caught and your fire truly begun to burn. To that end every true teacher must devote himself, and not count his work fairly begun till that is gained. When that is gained the scholar is richer by a new power of loving, the power of loving with his intellect, and he goes on through life, carrying in the midst of all the sufferings and disappointments which he meets a fountain of true joy in his own mind which can fill him with peace and happiness when men about him think that he has only dreariness and poverty and pain.

But now it is quite time to turn to Christ's commandment. I hope that we shall find that what we have been saying will make it clearer and stronger to us. Christ bids His disciples to love God with all their minds. As we hear His words we know that He is speaking for God. Near to God as He is in sympathy, one with God as He is in nature, we are sure that He is able to tell us what God wants of His children. And the glory of this part of His commandment, which we have chosen for our study, seems to me to be in this assurance which it gives us that God, the Father of men, is not satisfied if His children give Him simply gratitude for His mercies or the most loyal obedience to His will; but that He wants also, as the fulfilment of their love to Him, the enthusiastic use of their intellects, intent to know everything that it is possible for men to know about their Father and His ways. That is what, as I think we have seen, is meant by loving God with the mind. And is there not something sublimely beautiful and touching in this demand of God that the noblest part of His children's nature should come to Him? "Understand me! understand me!" He seems to cry; "I am not wholly loved by you unless your understanding is reaching out after my truth, and with all your powers of thoughtfulness and study you are trying to find out all that you can about my nature and my ways."

If we rightly interpret God when we seem to hear Him saying such words as these, then there must follow a conviction which certainly ought to bring comfort and incitement at once to many souls. It is that it is both man's privilege and duty to reason and think his best about God and the things of God, and that worse than any blunders or mistakes which any man may make in his religious thinking is the abandonment of religious thought altogether, and the consignment of the infinite interests of man to the mere region of feeling and emotion.

If you would know how needful that conviction is, you have only to listen to the strange way in which many people, both believers and unbelievers, talk about God and about religion. Hear what is the tone of many who call themselves believers. I go to a man who stands holding his Bible clasped with both hands upon his breast. I say to him, "Tell me about that book! What is it? Where did it come from? What is it made up of? How do its parts belong together? What is the ground of its authority? Why do you love it so?" And he turns round to me and says, "I will not ask, I will not hear questions like these! I love this book with all my heart! It has helped me. It has helped my fathers. When its promises speak to me I am calm. When its cry summons me I am brave. I will obey it and I will not question it. I love it with all my heart and soul and strength."

I see another man prostrate at the feet of God.

He knows that God is standing over him. He feels the shadow of the outstretched hand. He hears a voice which takes his will captive. I say to him, " Tell me about God. Try to explain to me what is His nature. Let me understand in some degree how He comes into communication with men's souls." And the grieved worshipper looks up almost in anger, and cries, " Away with such questions! You must not understand. You must not try to understand; you must only listen, and worship, and obey."

I see the soul which Christ has helped, the man for whom all the green earth is different because of the Divine feet that trod it once. I say to Him, " Let us see if we can know anything about the Incarnation. What has this coming of God among men in the wonderful life of His Son to do with that sonship of all men to God, which is an everlasting fact? How did He who came mean to deal with all the remote anticipations of His coming, and cravings after Him, of which the whole religious history of man is full? What were the wonderful works that fell from His hands, which we call miracles?" I ask such questions in the profoundest reverence; and again the lover of Christ turns off from me and says rebukingly, " You must not ask; Christ is above all questions. He bears His own witness to the soul

He helps. The less," even so some will speak of Him, "the less I understand of Him the more I love Him."

Yet once again I speak to the saint at His sacrament. I beg of him to let me know what that dear and lofty rite means to him; what are the perpetual faculties and dispositions of our human nature to which it appeals; how it is that he expects to receive his Saviour there. And he cries, "Hush! you must not rationalise. It is a mystery. No man can tell. The reason has no function here."

You will not misunderstand me, I am sure. You will not think that I disparage in the least degree the noble power of unreasoning love. The Bible, God, Christ, the Sacraments, the Church; these great realities cannot exist without finding out men's hearts, and winning them, and giving precious blessings through the adoration and emotion which they evoke. But what I want to say most earnestly is this, that each of the men I have described, with whatever other parts of himself he loves the object of his affection, does not love it with his mind; that, therefore, his affection is a crippled thing; and that if it be possible for him to bring his intelligence to bear upon his faith, to see the reasonableness which is at the heart of every truth, to discriminate between the true and the false forms of belief, to recognise how Christian truth is bound up with all the truth of which the world is full, and so to understand in some degree what now already he adores; he will, without losing in the least his adoration, gain a new delight in a perception of the beauty of his truth upon another side; his relation to it will be more complete; it will become more truly his; and his whole life will more completely feel its power.

There are Christians all about us who fear to bring their minds to bear upon their religion lest their hearts should lose their hold upon it. Surely there is something terrible in that. Surely it implies a terrible misgiving and distrust about their faith. They fear to think lest they should cease to love. But really it ought to be out of the heart of their thinking power that their deepest love is born. There is a love with most imperfect knowledge. The highest love which man can ever have for God must still live in the company of a knowledge which is so partial that, looked at against the perfect light, it will appear like darkness. But yet it still is true that the deeper is the knowledge the greater becomes the possibility of love. They always have loved God best, they are loving God best to-day, who gaze upon Him with wide-open eyes; who, conscious of their ignorance and weakness, more conscious of it the more they try to know, yet do try with all the powers He has given them, to understand all that they possibly can of Him and of His ways.

I said that the unbeliever as well as the believer needed to recognise, and often failed to recognise, the true place of the mind and thinking powers in religion. Let me tell you what I mean by that. There is a curious way of talking which seems to me to have grown strangely common of late among the men who disbelieve in Christianity. It is patronising, and quietly insulting; it takes for granted that the Christian's faith has no real reason at its heart, nor any trustworthy grounds for thinking itself true. At the same time it grants that there is a certain weak side of human nature, where the reason does not work, where everything depends on sentiment and feeling, where not what is true, but what is beautiful and comforting and reassuring is the soul's demand; and that side of the nature it gives over to religion. Because that side of the nature is the most prominent part, and indeed sometimes seems to be the whole, of weaker kinds of men and women, it accepts the necessity of religion for these weak people, and does not desire its immediate extinction; only it must not pretend to be a reasonable thing. Theology must not call itself a science, and Faith must know it is a dream. "Yes, be religious if you will," this spirit cries, "only do not imagine that your intellect has anything to do with it! Be religious; dwell on the beauty of the sacred past; let your lives walk in the twilight of imaginary cloisters; picture to yourselves what the world would be if there were a God; weep over the legendary woes of Jesus; dream of immortal life; give yourself up to rapturous emotions, whose source is largely physical; nay, if you will, be stirred by your dreams to noble and self-sacrificing work—do all this and be made happier. Yes, perhaps be made better—if there are such things as good and bad —by doing it; only, do not for a moment think that the mind, the reason, has anything to do with it at all. It is pure sentimentality. Religion is a thing of feelings and of fancies altogether." So pityingly, patronisingly, and insultingly talks many an unbeliever. Nay, strange as it may seem, there are some men whose minds are wholly sceptical of Christian truth, who yet allow themselves a sort of religion on the weaker side. They let their emotions be religious, while they keep their minds in the hard clear air of disbelief; the heart may worship, while the brain denies. I will not stop to ask the meaning of this last strange condition, interesting as the study might be made. I only want you all to feel how thoroughly Christianity is bound to reject indignantly this whole treatment of itself. Just think how the great masters of religion would receive it! Think of David and his cry—"Thy testimonies are wonderful. I have more understanding than my teachers, for thy testimonies are my study." Think of Paul—"O the depth of the riches both of the wisdom and knowledge of God." Think of Augustine, Luther, Calvin, Milton, Edwards, and a hundred more, the men whose minds have found their loftiest inspiration in religion, how would they have received this quiet and contemptuous relegation of the most stupendous subjects of human thought to the region of silly sentiment? They were men who loved the Lord their God with all their minds. The noble relation of their intellects to Him was the supreme satisfaction of their lives. We cannot imagine them for a moment as yielding up that great region of their lives in which their minds delighted in the study and attainment of His truth.

There are ignorant saints who come very near to God, and live in the rich sunlight of His love; but none the less for that is their ignorance a detraction from their sainthood. There are mystics who, seeing how God outgoes human knowledge, choose to assume that God is not a subject of human knowledge at all; that His works are distinct in kind from any of which we know, prompted by other motives, and proceeding upon principles entirely unintelligible to our reason. Such mystics may mount to sublime heights of unreasoning contemplation, but there is an incompleteness in their love ; because they rob one part of their nature of all share in their approach to God. Their first assumption is not true ; their starting-point is wrong. God's ways are not as our ways. More vast, infinitely more vast in size than ours, they stretch beyond us, as the ocean stretches beyond the little pool of water which it has left, separated from and yet united to itself, behind the extended arm of the outreaching shore. But yet, because we are made in the image of God, His ways are of the same kind as ours, and we may know very much about them as you may know much about the ocean from the study of the waters of the bay, and from the sight of how the tides sweep into it and out again. There is no principle involved in the Atonement of Christ that is not included in its essence in the most sacred relations between man and man. The Bible opens new beauties and depths to any man who studies its history, its geography, its language, with the same intelligence with which men study other books. The Church is an institution built of men, and a knowledge of human nature throws perpetual light upon its character and its hopes. Everywhere, to think that divine truth lies beyond or away from the intelligence of man, is at once to make divine truth unreal and unpractical, and to condemn the human intelligence to dealing not with the highest, but only with the lower themes.

I have pled with you to-day for the use of your intellects in matters of religion. By them you must discriminate between the false and the true. You have no other faculty with which to do that necessary work. You cannot know that one idea is necessarily true because it seems to help you, nor that another idea is false because it wounds and seems to hinder you. Your mind is your faculty for judging what is true; and only by the use of your thoughtful intellect, too, can you preserve your faith in the attacks which come against it on every side. However it may have been in other days, however it may seem to be to-day, in the days which are to come—the days in which the younger people who hear me now will live—there will be ever-increasing demand for thoughtful saints; for men and women, earnest, lofty, spiritual, but also full of intelligence, knowing the meaning and the reasons of the things which they believe, and not content to worship the God to whom they owe everything with less than their whole nature.

I appeal to you, young Christian people, to be ready for that coming time, with all its high demands. I appeal to you upon the highest grounds. Love God with all your mind, because your mind, like all the rest of you, belongs to Him, and it is not right that you should give Him only a part to whom belongs the whole. When the procession of your powers goes up joyfully singing to worship in the temple, do not leave the noblest of them all behind to cook the dinner and to tend the house. Give your intelligence to God. Know all that you can know about Him. In spite of all disappointment and weakness, insist on seeing all that you can see now through the glass darkly, so that hereafter you may be ready when the time for seeing face to face shall come!

May God stir some of us to-day to such ambition, to the consecration of our minds to Him!

III.

THE FIRE AND THE CALF.[1]

"So they gave it me: then I cast it into the fire and there came out this calf."—EXODUS xxxii. 24.

IN the story from which these words are taken we see Moses go up into the mountain to hold communion with God. While he is gone the Israelites begin to murmur and complain. They want other gods, gods of their own. Aaron, the brother of Moses, was their priest. He yielded to the people, and when they brought him their golden earrings he made out of them a golden calf for them to worship. When Moses came down from the mountain he found the people deep in their idolatry. He was indignant. First he destroyed the idol, " He burnt it in the fire, and ground it to powder, and strawed it upon the water, and made the children of Israel drink of it." Then he turned to Aaron. "What did

[1] Preached at Christ Church, Lancaster Gate, London, Sunday morning, 27th May 1883.

this people unto thee," he said, "that thou hast brought so great a sin upon them?" And Aaron meanly answered, "Let not the anger of my lord wax hot: thou knowest the people, that they are set on mischief. For they said unto me, Make us gods, which shall go before us.... And I said unto them, Whosoever hath any gold, let them break it off. So they gave it me: then I cast it into the fire, and there came out this calf." That was his mean reply. The real story of what actually happened had been written earlier in the chapter. When the people brought Aaron their golden earrings " he received them at their hand, and fashioned it with a graving tool, after he had made it a molten calf: and they said, These be thy gods, O Israel, which brought thee up out of the land of Egypt." That was what really happened, and this is the description which Aaron gave of it to Moses: " So they gave it me: then I cast it into the fire, and there came out this calf."

Aaron was frightened at what he had done. He was afraid of the act itself, and he was afraid of what Moses would say about it. Like all timid men, he trembled before the storm which he had raised. And so he tried to persuade Moses, and perhaps in some degree even to persuade himself, that it was not he that had done this thing. He lays the blame upon the furnace. "The fire did it," he declares. He will not blankly face his sin, and yet he will not tell a lie in words. He tells what is literally true. He had cast the earrings into the fire, and this calf had come out. But he leaves out the one important point, his own personal agency in it all; the fact that he had moulded the earrings into the calf's shape, and that he had taken it out and set it on its pedestal for the people to adore. He tells it so that it shall all look automatic. It is a curious, ingenious, but transparent lie.

Let us look at Aaron's speech a little while this morning, and see what it represents. For it does represent something. There never was a speech more true to one disposition of our human nature. We are all ready to lay the blame upon the furnaces. "The fire did it," we are all of us ready enough to say. Here is a man all gross and sensual, a man still young who has already lost the freshness and the glory and the purity of youth. He is profane; he is cruel; he is licentious; all his brightness has grown lurid; all his wit is ribaldry. You know the man. As far as a man can be, he is a brute. Suppose you question that man about his life. You expect him to be ashamed, to be repentant. There is not a sign of anything like that! He says, "I am the victim of circumstances. What a corrupt, licentious, profane age this is in which we live! When I was in college I got into a bad set. When I went into business I was surrounded by bad influences. When I grew rich, men flattered me. When I grew poor, men bullied me. The world has made me what I am, this fiery, passionate, wicked world. I had in my hands the gold of my boyhood which God gave me. Then I cast it into the fire, and there came out this calf." And so the poor wronged miserable creature looks into your face with his bleared eyes and asks your pity. Another man is not a profligate, but is a miser, or a mere business machine. "What can you ask of me," he says, "this is a mercantile community. The business man who does not attend to his business goes to the wall. I am what this intense commercial life has made me. I put my life in there, and it came out this." And then he gazes fondly at his golden calf, and his knees bend under him with the old long habit of worshipping it, and he loves it still, even while he abuses and disowns it. And so with the woman of society. "The fire made me this," she says of her frivolity and pride. And so of the politician and his selfishness and partisanship. "I put my principles into the furnace, and this came out." And so of the bigot and his bigotry, the one-sided conservative with his stubborn resistance to all progress, the one-sided radical with his ruthless iconoclasm. So of all partial and fanatical men. "The furnace made us," they are ready to declare. "These times compel us to be this. In better times we might have been better, broader men; but now, behold, God put us into the fire, and we came out this." It is what one is perpetually hearing about disbelief. "The times have made me sceptical. How is it possible for a man to live in days like these and yet believe in God and Jesus and the Resurrection. You ask me how I, who was brought up in the faith and in the Church, became a disbeliever. Oh, you remember that I lived five years here," or "three years there." "You know I have been very much thrown with this set or with that. You know the temper of our town. I cast myself into the fire, and I came out this." One is all ready to understand, my friends, how the true soul, struggling for truth, seems often to be worsted in the struggle. One is ready to have tolerance, respect, and hope for any man who, reaching after God, is awed by God's immensity and his own littleness, and falls back crushed and doubtful. His is a doubt which is born in the secret chambers of his own personal conscientiousness. It is independent of his circumstances and surroundings. The soul which has truly come to a personal doubt finds it hard to conceive of any ages of most implicit faith in which it could have lived in which that doubt would not have been in it. It faces its doubt in a solitude where there is none but it and God. All that one understands, and the more he understands it the more unintelligible does it seem to him, that any earnest soul can really lay its doubt upon the age, the set, or the society it lives in. No; our age, our society is what, with this figure taken out of the old story of Exodus, we have been calling it. It is the furnace. Its fire can set and fix and fasten what the man puts into it. But, properly speaking, it can create no character. It can make no truly faithful soul a doubter. It never did. It never can.

Remember that the subtlety and attractiveness of this excuse, this plausible attributing of power to inanimate things and exterior conditions to create what only man can make, extends not only to the results which we see coming forth in ourselves; it covers also the fortunes of those for whom we are responsible. The father says of his profligate son whom he has never done one wise or vigorous thing to make a noble and pure-minded man: "I cannot tell how it has come. It has not been my fault. I put him into the world and this came out." The father whose faith has been mean and selfish says the same of his boy who is a sceptic. Everywhere there is this cowardly casting off of responsibilities upon the dead circumstances around us. It is a very hard treatment of the poor, dumb, helpless world which cannot answer to defend itself. It takes us as we give ourselves to it. It is our minister fulfilling our commissions for us upon our own souls. If we say to it, "Make us noble," it does make us noble. If we say to it, "Make us mean," it does make us mean. And then we take the nobility and say, "Behold, how noble I have made myself." And we take the meanness and say, "See how mean the world has made me."

You see, I am sure, how perpetual a thing the temper of Aaron is, how his excuse is heard everywhere and always. I need not multiply illustrations. But now, if all the world is full of it, the next question is, What does it mean? Is it mere pure deception, or is there also delusion, self-deception in it? Take Aaron's case. Was he simply telling a lie to Moses and trying to hide the truth from his brother whom he dreaded, when he said, "I cast the earrings into the fire, and this calf came out"? Or was he in some dim degree, in some half-conscious way, deceiving himself? Was he allowing himself to attribute some power to the furnace in the making of the calf? Perhaps as we read the verse above in which it is so distinctly said that Aaron fashioned the idol with a graving tool, any such supposition seems incredible. But yet I cannot but think that some degree, however dim, of such self-deception was in Aaron's heart. The fire was mysterious. He was a priest. Who could say that some strange creative power had not been at work there in the heart of the furnace which had done for him what he seemed to do for himself. There was a human heart under that ancient ephod, and it is hard to think that Aaron did not succeed in bringing himself to be somewhat imposed upon by his own words, and hiding his responsibility in the heart of the hot furnace. But however it may have been with Aaron, there can be no doubt that in almost all cases this is so. Very rarely indeed does a man excuse himself to other men and yet remain absolutely unexcused in his own eyes. When Pilate stands washing the responsibility of Christ's murder from his hands before the people, was he not feeling himself as if his hands grew cleaner while he washed? When Shakespeare paints Macbeth with the guilty ambition which was to be his ruin first rising in his heart, you remember how he makes him hide his newborn purpose to be king even from himself, and pretend that he believes that he is willing to accept the kingdom only if it shall come to him out of the working of things, for which he is not responsible, without an effort of his own.

"If chance will have me king, why, chance may crown me,
Without my stir."

That was the first stage of the growing crime which finally was murder. Often it takes this form. Often the very way to help ourselves most to a result which we have set before ourselves is just to put ourselves into a current which is sweeping on that way, and then lie still and let the current do the rest; and in all such cases it is so easy to ignore or to forget the first step, which was that we chose that current for our resting-place, and so to say that it is only the drift of the current which is to blame for the dreary shore on which at last our lives are cast up by the stream. Suppose you are to-day a scornful man, a man case-hardened in conceit and full of disbelief in anything generous or supernatural, destitute of all enthusiasm, contemptuous, supercilious. You say the time you live in has made you so. You point to one large tendency in the community which always sets that way. You parade the specimens of enthusiastic people whom you have known who have been fanatical and silly. You tell me what your favourite journal has been saying in your ears every week for years. You bid me catch the tone of the brightest people whom you live among, and then you turn to me and say, " How could one live in such an atmosphere and not grow cynical ? Behold, my times have made me what I am." What does that mean ? Are you merely trying to hide from me, or are you also hiding from yourself, the certain fact that you have chosen that special current to launch your boat upon, that you have given your whole attention to certain kinds of facts and shut your eyes to certain others, that you have constantly valued the brightness which went to the depreciation of humanity and despised the urgency with which a healthier, spirit has argued for the good in man and for his everlasting hope ? Is it not evident that you yourself have been able to half forget all this, and so when the stream on which you launched your boat at last drives it upon the beach to which it has been flowing all the time, there is a certain lurking genuineness in the innocent surprise with which you look around upon the desolate shore on which you land, and say to yourself, " How unhappy I am that I should have fallen upon these evil days, in which it is impossible that a man should genuinely respect or love his fellowmen " ?

For there are currents flowing always in all

bad directions. There is a perpetual river flowing towards sensuality and vice. There is a river flowing perpetually towards hypocrisy and religious pretence. There is a river always running towards scepticism and infidelity. And when you once have given yourself up to either of these rivers, then there is quite enough in the continual pressure, in that great movement like a fate beneath your keel, to make you lose the sense and remembrance that it is by your own will that you are there, and only think of the resistless flow of the river which is always in your eyes and ears. This is the mysterious, bewildering mixture of the consciousness of guilt and the consciousness of misery in all our sin. We live in a perpetual confusion of self-pity and self-blame. We go up to the scaffolds where we are to suffer, half like culprits crawling to the gallows and half like martyrs proudly striding to their stakes. When we think of what sort of reception is to meet us in the other world as the sum and judgment of the life we have been living here, we find ourselves ready, according to the moment's mood, either for the bitterest denunciation, as of souls who have lived in deliberate sin; or for tender petting and refreshment, as of souls who have been buffeted and knocked about by all the storms of time, and for whom now there ought to be soft beds in eternity.

The confusion of men's minds about the judgments of the eternal world is only the echo of their confusion about the responsibilities of the life which they are living now.

Suppose there is a man here this morning who committed a fraud in business yesterday. He did it in a hurry. He did not stop to think about it then. But now, here, in this quiet church, with everything calm and peaceful round him, with the words of prayer which have taken God for granted sinking into his ears, he has been thinking it over. How does it look to him? Is he not certainly sitting in the mixture of self-pity and self-reproach of which I spoke? He did the sin, and he is sorry as a sinner. The sin did itself, and he is sorry as a victim. Nay, perhaps in the next pew to him, or perhaps in the same pew, or perhaps in the same body, there is sitting a man who means to do a fraud to-morrow. In him too is there not the same confusion? One moment he looks it right in the face and says, "To-morrow night I shall despise myself." The next moment he is quietly thinking that the sin will do itself and give him all its advantage, and he need not interfere

"If chance will make me cheat, why, chance may crown me,
Without my stir."

Both thoughts are in his mind, and if he has

listened to our service, it is likely enough that he has found something in it—something even in the words of the Bible—for each thought to feed upon.

I own this freely, and yet I do believe, and I call you to bear me witness, that such self-deception almost never is absolutely complete. We feel its incompleteness the moment that any one else attempts to excuse us with the same excuse with which we have excused ourselves. Suppose that some one of the Israelites who stood by had spoken up in Aaron's behalf and said to Moses, "Oh, he did not do it. It was not his act. He only cast the gold into the fire, and there came out this calf." Must not Aaron as he listened have felt the wretchedness of such a telling of the story, and been ashamed, and even cried out and claimed his responsibility and his sin? Very often it is good for us to imagine some one saying aloud in our behalf what we are silently saying to ourselves in self-apology. We see its thinness when another hand holds it up against the sun, and we stand off and look at it. If I might turn again to Shakespeare and his wonderful treasury of human character, there is a scene in Hamlet which exactly illustrates what I mean. The king has determined that Hamlet must die, and is just sending him off upon the voyage from which he means that he is never to return. And the king has fully explained the act to his own conscience, and accepted the crime as a necessity. And then he meets the courtiers, Rosencrantz and Guildenstern, who are to have the execution of the base commission. And they, like courtiers, try to repeat to the king the arguments with which he has convinced himself. One says—

> "Most holy and religious fear it is
> To keep those many many bodies safe
> That live and feed upon your majesty."

And the other takes up the strain and says—

> "The single and peculiar life is bound,
> With all the strength and armour of the mind,
> To keep itself from 'noyance; but much more
> That spirit upon whose weal depend and rest
> The lives of many."

They are the king's own arguments. With them he has persuaded his own soul to tolerate the murder. But when they come to him from these other lips, he will none of them. He cuts them short. He cannot hear from others what he has said over and over to himself.

> "Arm you, I pray you, to this speedy voyage."

So he cries out and interrupts them. Let the deed be done, but let not these echoes of his self-excuse parade before him the way in which he is trifling with his own soul.

So it is always. I think of the mysterious judgment-day, and sometimes it appears to me as if our souls would need no more than merely that voices outside ourselves should utter in our ears the very self-same pleas and apologies with which we, here upon the earth, have extenuated our own wickedness. They of themselves, heard in the open air of eternity, would let us see how weak they were, and so we should be judged. Is not that partly the reason why we hate the scene of some old sin? The room in which we did it seems to ring for ever with the sophistries by which we persuaded ourselves that it was right, and will not let us live in comfortable delusion. Our life there is an anticipated judgment-day.

I doubt not that this tendency to self-deception and apology with reference to the sins which they commit differs exceedingly with different men. Men differ, perhaps, nowhere else more than in their disposition to face the acts of their lives and to recognise their own personal part in and responsibility for the things they do. Look, for instance, at this Aaron and his brother Moses. The two men are characterised and illustrated by their two sins. The sin of Aaron was a denial or concealment of his own personal agency. "I cast it into the fire, and there came out this calf." The sin of Moses, you remember, was just the opposite.

As he stood with his thirsty people in front of the rock in Horeb, he intruded his personal agency where it had no right. "Hear now, ye rebels; must we fetch you water out of this rock?" To be sure, in the case of Moses it was a good act of mercy to which he put in his claim, while in Aaron's case it was a wicked act whose responsibility he desired to avoid. And men are always ready to claim the good deeds in which they have the smallest share, even when they try to disown the sins which are entirely their own. But still the actions seem to mark the men. Moses is the franker, manlier, braver man. In Aaron the priest there is something in that oversubtle, artificial, complicated character, that power of becoming morally confused even in the midst of pious feeling, that lack of simplicity, and of the disposition to look things frankly in the eye; in a word, that vague and defective sense of personality and its responsibilities which has often in the history of religion made the very name of priestcraft a reproach. Moses is the prophet. His distinct mission is the utterance of truth. He is always simple; never more simple than when he is most profound; never more sure of the fundamental principles of right and wrong, of honesty and truth, than when he is deepest in the mystery of God; never more conscious of himself and his responsibilities than when he is most conscious of God and His power.

And this brings me to my last point, which I must not longer delay to reach. If the world is thus full of the Aaron spirit, of the disposition to throw the blame of wrong-doing upon other things and other people, to represent to others, and to our own souls, that our sins do themselves, what is the real spiritual source of such a tendency, and where are we to look to find its cure? I have just intimated what seems to me to be its source. It is a vague and defective sense of personality. Anything which makes less clear to a man the fact that he, standing here on his few inches of the earth, is a distinct separate being, in whom is lodged a unit of life, with his own soul, his own character, his own chances, his own responsibilities, distinct and separate from any other man's in all the world; anything that makes all that less clear demoralises a man, and opens the door to endless self-excuses. And you know, surely, how many tendencies there are to-day which are doing just that for men. Every man's personality, his clear sense of himself, seems to be standing to-day where almost all the live forces of the time are making their attacks upon it. It is like a tree in the open field from which every bird carries away some fruit. The enlargement of our knowledge of the world, the growing tendency of men to work in large companies, the increased despotism of social life, the interesting studies of hereditation, the externality of a large part of our action, the rush and competition for the prizes which represent the most material sort of success, the spread of knowledge by which at once all men are seen to know much, and, at the same time, no man is seen to know everything; all these causes enfeeble the sense of personality. The very prominence of the truth of a universal humanity, in which our philanthropy justly glories, obscures the clearness of the individual human life. Once it was hard to conceive of man, because the personalities of men were so distinct. Once people found it hard, as the old saying was, to see the forest for the trees. Now it is just the opposite. To hundreds of people it is almost impossible to see the trees for the forest. Man is so clear that men become obscure. As the Laureate of the century sings of the time which he so well knows: "The individual withers and the race is more and more." These are the special causes, working in our time, of that which has its general causes in our human nature working everywhere and always.

And if this is the trouble, where, then, is the help? If this is the disease, where is the cure?

I cannot look for it anywhere short of that great assertion of the human personality which is made when a man personally enters into the power of Jesus Christ. Think of it! Here is some Aaron of our modern life trying to cover up some sin which he has done. The fact of the sin is clear enough. There is no possibility of concealing that. It stands out wholly undisputed. It is not by denying that the thing was done but by beclouding the fact that he did it with his own hands, with his own will; thus it is that the man would cover up his sin. He has been nothing but an agent, nothing but a victim; so he assures his fellowmen, so he assures himself. And now suppose that while he is doing that, the great change comes to that man by which he is made a disciple and servant of Jesus Christ. It becomes known to him as a certain fact that God loves him individually, and is educating him with a separate personal education which is all his own. The clear individuality of Jesus stands distinctly out and says to him, " Follow me!" Jesus stops in front of where he is working just as evidently, with just as manifest intention of calling him as that with which He stopped in front of the booth where Matthew was sitting collecting taxes, and says, " Follow me." He is called separately, and separately he does give himself to Christ. Remember all that is essential to a Christian faith. You cannot blur it all into indistinctness and generality. In the true light of the redeeming Incarnation, every man in the multitude stands out as every blade of grass on the hillside stands distinct from every other when the sun has risen. In this sense, as in many another, this is the true light which lighteneth every man that cometh into the world.

The Bible calls it a new birth, and in that name too there are many meanings. And among other meanings in it must there not be this—the separateness and personality of every soul in Christ? Birth is the moment of distinctness. The meanest child in the poorest hovel in the city, who by and by is to be lost in the great whirlpool of human life, here at the outset where his being comes, a new fact, into the crowded world, is felt in his distinctness, has his own personal tending, excites his own personal emotion. When he is born and when he dies, but perhaps most of all when he is born, the commonest, most commonplace and undistinguished of mankind asserts the fact of privilege of his separateness. And so when the possession of the soul by Christ is called the "New Birth," one of the meanings of that name is this, that then there is a reassertion of personality, and the soul which had lost itself in the slavery of the multitude finds itself again in the obedience of Christ.

And now what will be the attitude of this man, with his newly-awakened selfhood, towards that sin which he has been telling himself that his hands did, but that he did not do? May we not almost say that he will need that sin for his self-identification? Who is he? A being whom Christ has forgiven, and then in virtue of that forgiveness made His servant. All his new life dates from and begins with his sin. He cannot afford to find his consciousness of himself only in the noble parts of his life, which it makes him proud and happy to remember. There is not enough of that to make for him a complete and continuous personality. It will have great gaps if he disowns the wicked demonstrations of his selfhood and says, "It was not I," wherever he has done wrong. No! Out of his sin, out of the bad, base, cowardly acts which are truly his, out of the weak and wretched passages of his life which it makes him ashamed to remember, but which he forces himself to recollect and own, out of these he gathers the consciousness of a self all astray with self-will which he then brings to Christ and offers in submission and obedience to His perfect will.

You try to tell some soul rejoicing in the Lord's salvation that the sins over whose forgiveness by its Lord it is gratefully rejoicing, were not truly its; and see what strange thing comes. The soul seems to draw back from your assurance as if, if it were true, it would be robbed of all its surest confidence and brightest hope. You meant to comfort the poor penitent, and he looks into your face as if you were striking him a blow. And you can see what such a strange sight means. It is not that the poor creature loves those sins or is glad that he did them, or dreams for an instant of ever doing them again. It is only that through those sins, which are all the real experience he has had, he has found himself, and finding himself has found his Saviour and the new life.

So the only hope for any of us is in a perfectly honest manliness to claim our sins. "I did it, I did it," let me say of all my wickedness. Let me refuse to listen for one moment to any voice which would make my sins less mine. It is the only honest and the only hopeful way, the only way to know and be ourselves. When we have done that, then we are ready for the Gospel, ready for all that Christ wants to show us that we may become, and for all the powerful grace by which He wants to make us be it perfectly.

IV.

MAN'S WONDER AND GOD'S KNOWLEDGE.[1]

"Thus saith the Lord of hosts: If it be marvellous in the eyes of the remnant of this people in these days, should it also be marvellous in mine eyes? saith the Lord of hosts."—ZECHARIAH viii. 6.

THIS is a very wonderful age in which we live. So men are constantly in the habit of saying to each other. So, no doubt, men have always said about their ages. There can hardly ever have been a time which to the men who lived in it did not seem full of emphatic and remarkable differences which distinguished it from all other times, and made it very wonderful and strange. But there is a second sense in which the familiar words might be used, in which no doubt they would peculiarly describe our time. It is a wonderful age not merely in the number of strange unprecedented things which are happening in it, the

[1] Preached in Westminster Abbey, Sunday evening, 27th May 1883.

strange unprecedented character that belongs to it as a whole, but also in the prominence of wonder as an element in the view which it takes of itself. It is a wonderful age, because it is an age full of wonder. It does not seem as if there ever can have been a time which so stood off and looked at itself, as it were; a time in which so many men lived under the continual sense of the strangeness of their own circumstances; a time when it entered as such a large element into the formation of the character of a century that that century considered itself to be exceptional and new, unexplained by the centuries which have preceded it, and quite vague as to the results that must follow it in the centuries to come. You will see at once how important such an element must be in the character of any age which possesses it if you remember what it is in an individual. A child who thinks himself singular and different from other children grows up under the power of that thought more than of any other that is in his mind. The kind of effect which it will have on him will depend upon the essential nature he possesses. It will differ very greatly in different children. It will make one child timid and another bold, but always it will be the most effective of all the child's thoughts. And so the age which is always saying to itself, "How strange I am! how new! how different from all the ages which have gone before! how bewildering! how surprising!" will carry in that pervading wonder the quality which will influence the characters of the men who live in it more than any other. No doubt according to their different natures the influence is always various. One man's wonder is delight, and another man's is consternation. One man, the more he wonders, is inspired with hope; another man sees in the mystery about him nothing but fear. To one man the wonderfulness of his age, its wonderful inventions, wonderful thoughts, wonderful audacity, wonderful mastery of the earth, wonderful types of human character, is a constantly elevating, refining, mellowing power; to another it is a perpetual paralysis. Some men are made great and brought to their very best; other men are ruined by it. But whatever be the kind of its effect, it is an element in the life and growth of every man, this wonder at the age he lives in, at the world, at men, and at himself; this wonder which everywhere pervades our own wonderful age.

And what is the reason that this sense of the wonderfulness of life, this sense of strangeness and mystery everywhere, has such different effects upon different men, brings one man peace and another tumult, brings hope to one and despair to another? No doubt the reason lies deep in the essential differences that there are between our natures, and cannot wholly be stated. But one cause of the difference, and not the least one, lies here, in the difference of our ideas as to whether there is any being who knows what we are every hour reminded that we do not know, any being in whose eyes this which is strange to us is not strange or bewildering, but perfectly natural and orderly and clear. Two men alike are in the spirit of their time; they both are men of wonder; they both confess their ignorance; they both stand marvelling at the quick changes which are flashing all around them, and at the dim mysterious infinity into which the simplest things around them stretch away and where their sight is lost. So far they are alike. But now to one of those men it has been shown, flashed from some sudden lightning which has blazed out of the cloud, or dawning slowly to him out of the very substance of the cloud itself, out of something in the very bosom of the mystery which met the mystery in his own heart and spoke to it in some way; it has been shown to one of them that there is a Mind which knows what he is so hopelessly powerless to know; there is a God to whom this strange bewilderment is not strange. Somewhere there is an eye which looks on all this and feels no wonder, because it looks it through and through and sees its first principles and final causes clear as daylight. The other man knows nothing of all this. To him the wonder that his own mind feels runs everywhere. The world is a great snarl and mystery not merely to him but to every intelligence which he conceives of. He is like a sailor on a ship that has no captain. Not merely he does not know where the ship is going; nobody knows; at least nobody knows whom he knows. Is it not clear how vast the difference must be? To the one man the darkness is all palpitating with light, the light of a knowledge behind it, the light of God, in whom is no darkness at all. This man's very ignorance becomes the element in him to which God manifests Himself. Through that low and dark door he enters the great high vaulted world of faith. His wonder is the atmosphere through which the sun shines on him. The other man carries his wonder as the earth would carry a cloud if there were no sun, first to shine through it and then to promise that it shall ultimately scatter. It cannot help crushing him when in his doubt he knows of no intelligence to which that which is dark to him is bright. He is all helpless in the present, and the future has no promise of escape. Oh, my dear friends, we are too ready to think that God is surprised with this endless surprise and strangeness which come to us in life. Our only hope of strength and peace lies in knowing that there is one whom nothing disappoints and nothing amazes. He was not disappointed when the good man died; he was not amazed when thought took such and such a sudden turn and such or such a heresy broke out. Unless we are sure of that our disappointment or amazement must overwhelm us. Wonder is so thoroughly a part of ourselves, and such a constant experience, that we can hardly leave out wonder from our thought of any nature, but we know that from the completest nature it must be left out, and some sublime peace of omniscience, totally unknown to us, must come in in its place to make the perfect joy of God.

It is high time to turn to our text. Zechariah, speaking to the Jews in their captivity, has been foretelling the restoration of Jerusalem. Some day the great dear sacred city is to shine again upon its holy mountain. It is to be splendid with prosperity and sweet with peace. All the signs of contentment and comfort shall be seen there. "There shall yet old men and old women dwell in the streets of Jerusalem, and every man with his staff in his hand for very age. And the streets of the city shall be full of boys and girls playing in the streets thereof." And then, as if he turned and saw incredulity upon the faces of the poor prisoners in Babylon, he cries, " Thus saith the Lord of hosts, If it be marvellous in the eyes of the remnant of this people, shall it also be marvellous in my eyes? saith the Lord of hosts." I do not want to preach about the special promise which Zechariah brought, but you see how in the strong remonstrance with which he meets their incredulity there is the substance of all that I have thus far been saying. "It is all strange to you," God by His prophet says to the captives. "Does that prove that it is strange to me? You wonder and cannot believe. Do you think I do not see deeper than you do? There are things which to you are strange which to me are wholly natural. You must not limit my knowledge by your wonder, for if you do how can I give you that richer knowledge which I want to give you through the higher medium of faith?"

I do not want to dwell upon the special story, but only to catch its general idea and see what it means for us. Where we are ignorant, God is wise; where we stand blindly in the dark, He is in the light; where we wonder, He calmly knows. "God knows," we sometimes say in a light and flippant tone when some one asks us a question that is too hard for us. "What will become of us in these hard times?" one poor man says to another, and the answer is, "God knows." "Where is our country drifting?" ponder two patriots, and they turn away from one another's ignorance with no other light to give each other but just, "Well, God knows." If the words have any true reality they ought to bring the same sort of comfort which Zechariah was trying to give to the captive Hebrews when he said, "If it be marvellous in your eyes, shall it also be marvellous in my eyes? saith the Lord of hosts."

When we ask what that comfort is, I think we find it really comprehended under two words. The first is *safety*, the second is *enlargement*. These words describe two needs of every man's life, and these two needs both find their supply in the assurance that what are wonders and mysteries to us are wholly clear to God, within whose life our life is held. Let me speak of the two in order.

1. Remember, then, where so much of the sense of danger, the sense of unsafety, in life comes from. It is not from the things that we see and have known all along, it is from the half-seen forms which hover just upon the borders of reality and unreality—things which evidently are something, but of which we cannot perfectly make out just what they are. At sea, it is not the ship whose shape you perfectly discern, and all whose movements you can follow; it is the ship that hovers like a dim ghost in the fog, moved by an

unseen hand—evidently there, but vague and mysterious; that is the ship of which you fear lest any moment it may strike you. And so (for I am thinking specially about the dangers that beset faith, the dangers of which every thoughtful man or woman is aware in these strange days of ours), it is not the ideas that have been proved as truths and which have taken their places as distinctly-seen parts of human knowledge, it is not those that in these days are making men tremble for their own or for the world's religious faith. Indeed, nothing is more wonderful than to see how, just as soon as any idea has received demonstration, religious faith has always found a place for it, perhaps with some modification of some of the statements which she had made about herself before, but always with a cordial welcome which took the new proved truth into her structure and made it even a buttress or pillar of her strength. It is not these, not the clear-seen and certain truths, which frighten men for the stability of faith. It is the ghostly speculations, the vaguely-outlined suggestions which hover in the misty lights of dim hypothesis. It is the forms which peer out of the just-opened, not yet explored chambers of new sciences. It is the visions which are painted in the glowing words of the poets among the scientists of what their sciences have not yet done, but what they dream that they may do some day,—these are the things which make the dim uneasy sense of danger which besets the minds of Christian believers. Unknown, before unguessed intimacies of connection between the body and the soul of man ; and, corresponding to this, before unguessed relationships between the higher and the lower orders of created life ; these are examples of the suggested truths which make men fear for faith. I cannot say how such suggestions may strike other men, but to me the case seems to be this. In the first place, the ultimate result of every deeper insight into the orderliness of nature, however for a time it may seem to stop the inquirer's inquiry short at the fact of order, as if that were a final thing, must be to make more certain the existence of an orderer, to make mankind more sure of God. And if I only can keep sure of Him, then, since His very essence is omniscience, no revelation with regard to His great world can startle or bewilder me, or give me for one moment any thought of danger. Behind all my conceptions and all other men's conceptions of what things are and how they came to be, there always must lie the true fact about things, about what they are and how they came to be. That fact, again, must correspond exactly with the knowledge of the fact which is in the supreme intelligence of Him who knows all things exactly and completely. If my conception of the fact, however it was reached, differs to-day from His knowledge of the fact, danger must lie in the persistence of that difference, and not in its being set right. Ignorance is always dangerous, knowledge never is. If any so-called discovery which men are teaching me to-day is really true, God has known it all along. However marvellous it is to me, it is not marvellous to Him. He knew it when He made the mind of man with its capacity of faith and of religion. And now, when He sees you and me trembling for fear lest such or such a theory may gather so much evidence that we cannot reject it, but will have to own it to be true, it seems to be that I can almost feel His presence bending over us and hear Him say, " My children, if it be true, do you not want to believe it? I have known it all along. By coming to the truth you come to me, who have held the truth in my bosom—nay, by whom the truth is true. Do not be frightened. I cannot be taken by surprise. If it be marvellous in the eyes of the remnant of this people, should it also be marvellous in my eyes." When a man has once heard that voice of God, then there seems to him only one safe, prudent, cautious thing to do, which is to look and listen everywhere for well-proved truth, however new and unexpected, and to take it with a cordial welcome wherever it is found.

I would not have you think, my friends, that I am thinking only of the things about which scholars and theologians are puzzling their minds. To all of you there come new discoveries even in the most common things. You find that some opinion which you have thought all wrong has in it some precious elements of truth. You find that some man whom you thought a poor fool, or a base deceiver, is really noble, generous, self-sacrificing, wise. You find that some Church which you despised as irregular, or condemned with still bitterer contempt as vulgar and unrefined, is really doing sterling work for God and man. You find that the plan for your soul's education, which you have laid out and taken for granted, is going to prove impossible. Tell me, will it not help you to accept the new knowledge cordially?—will it not let you escape from your prejudice, and see, not merely that it is safe for you to accept the new knowledge, but also that it is totally unsafe to refuse to accept it, if you can remember that God has known it all along, and therefore that, in letting go your prejudice and cordially stepping forth into the new light, you are coming nearer to Him? He who values truth only as the way to God, he who counts his opinions valueless except as they agree with the infallible judgments of God, and so bring him who holds them into the sympathy of God and keeps him there, he is the man for whom all life is safe, and whose quiet faith faces the changing thoughts and fortunes of the world without a fear.

2. And then, to pass on to our second point, such a man also is free. I have been speaking of this already, for our two points are not so distinct from one another as they seemed. The safety of life and the enlargement or freedom of life must go together. No man is safe who is not free. No man is free who is not safe. But let us turn our thoughts now to this point of the enlargement of a man's life who always feels behind and around his own ignorance the perfect knowledge of God. Our efforts, our action—indeed our whole life of thought and will—is limited by that which we count possible. Only a dreamer busies his brain and wastes his time on that which he believes to be for ever impossible, by its very nature, for any being to do. But it is evident enough that the conception of what is possible enlarges and widens as the quality of being becomes higher; and so the loftier being is able freely to attempt things which the lower being is shut out from if he lives only in the contemplation of his own powers, and does not look beyond himself. A great man comes and stands, like Moses, before a nation of slaves, and

says, "I will lead you out of your bondage." "It is impossible," comes the answer back from each crushed and broken spirit. Another great man stands on the beach of the uncrossed ocean and says, "I will sail across it, and find land upon the other side." Again the answer rises from a whole unenterprising world, "It is impossible." Another great man says, "The Church is all corrupt; her sins must be defied, and she must be reformed!" Another cries out at the thought of a nation growing up in ignorance, and says, "Each child must go to school." To all of them the mass of men answer, "Impossible!" And the reply which the great, bold men make by their lives, if not by their lips, is always the same—"To you it may be impossible, but it is not to me; if it be marvellous in your eyes, should it also be in mine?" And soon the slaves are marching out of their bondage with songs, and the ship is sailing westward through the unknown seas, and the reformation has begun, and the school-houses are blossoming all over the land. Do you not see the freedom to attempt which belongs to the larger vision? And do you not see also that this freedom to attempt is something which cannot be confined to the great men who see the visions first? When once a great deed has proclaimed the possibility, a hundred little ships put out from shore; a hundred little arms are raised to strike the giant wrong. And do you not see, most of all, that if He who sits at the centre of everything, and sees the visions of the universe with the perfect clearness of its Maker—if God can really speak and say, "It seems impossible to you, but it is not impossible; it is marvellous in your eyes, but not in mine"—if He can say that of any task which is overwhelming men with its immensity, that word of His must set free the little strength of all of us to strike our little blows, must enlarge our lives, and send them out to bolder ventures with earnestness and hope.

This seems to me to be what Jesus was always doing. Do you remember how often He said to His disciples such words as "Marvel not at this," or, "With man this is impossible, but with God all things are possible"? He was opening new regions for men's hope and action by surrounding their ignorance with the knowledge of His Father. To how many a poor soul, then, and in the ages since, who had dared say no more than, "I will try to earn my dinner, because I know that power is in me," Jesus has spoken and said, "Nay, but you must try to be good, strong, useful, unselfish; you must try to save your soul, because the God whose child you are, the God whom I show to you, knows that that power is in you"?

There is no end to the illustrations of this idea. Let me select two or three, and speak of them very briefly. Suppose a man has dared to do what men, good and religious men, are always doing: he has tied the fortunes of faith and religion to some special statement of doctrine or some special organisation of religious life. A man has dared to say that some one of the temporary means of faith is essential to the existence of faith upon the earth. No matter what it is. One man says, An infallible Church; another man says, This theory of inspiration; another man says, Subscriptions and assuring oaths; another man says, The Bible in the public schools; another man says, A loyal belief in everlasting punishment—every man has his test and condition. "Without this," he says, "faith is impossible." Oh, my dear friends, it seems to me sometimes as if, through all these ages of Christendom, God had been trying to teach the Christian world to enlarge its notion of the possibilities of faith by the perpetual revelation of His own. It seems to me to-day that God must be teaching us all that faith, the essential relation of the human soul to His soul, the deep rest of the child's life on the Father's life; faith, the reception by man of the Word of God, which comes to him in voices as manifold as is the nature of God Himself; that faith, a thing so deep, essential, and eternal, is not to be conditioned on the permanence of any one of the temporary forms in which it may be clothed. If the future is like the past, men will come to disbelieve many things which they believe now, and yet they will keep faith in God; men will come to believe many things which they disbelieve now, and yet they will keep faith in God. The earnest believer says, "I do not see how that can be; it is too strange;" but God answers him out of all history—"If it is marvellous in your eyes, must it also be marvellous in mine?" Only he who consents to enlarge his own conception of the possibilities of faith with God's can calmly watch the everlasting growth of revelation, see the old open into the new, and yet know that the truth of Christ is the truth of eternity, and that when the soul of God claimed the soul of man in the Incarnation, it took possession of it for ever; and so Christian faith can never die.

There have been no nobler servants of God and of humanity than they whose special mission it has been to teach this truth to men. You will forgive me if, standing here to-night, I pause one instant as I pass to name with reverence and love him who, for ever associated with these venerable walls, must also stand for ever in the minds of those who knew his life and work as the brave, enthusiastic, devoted apostle of the freedom of faith, the freedom of the faithful man who feels for ever behind his own ignorance the certainty of God. To discriminate between the eternal substance of Christianity and its temporary forms, to bid men see how often forms had perished and the substance still survived, to make men know the danger of imperfect and false tests of faith, to encourage them to be not merely resigned but glad as they beheld the one faith ever casting its old forms away, and by its undying vitality creating for itself new—this was the noble work which Dean Stanley did for multitudes of grateful souls all over Christendom. He led countless hearts out of the surprise and fear of their own day into the unsurprised and fearless peace of faith in God. Thus it was that he opened wide the great gates of the Divine Life, and made the way more clear for the children to their Father.

Turn, then, to another illustration. What great light our truth throws upon the prospects of a deepened spiritual life for Christendom. If we look around upon the Christian world in the midst of which we live, the sight seems sometimes very strange. It seems as if religious men had come deliberately to the conviction that only a very moderate degree of consecration, of enthusiasm, of missionary zeal, of seeking after holiness were possible in our condition. The Church is secular. The Christian snatches a few moments for his prayer, and then he drowns the whole long day in business. The "religious public" lives not like a leaven in the great community; rather it is like a bit of ornamental decoration stuck on the outside of the great solid loaf. Men have forgotten how to lift up their voices in the assemblies of their fellow-men and tell what God has done for them, or to cry out to Him with eager prayer. Enthusiasm about the most infinite and exalting things in all the universe has well-nigh gone. You know the picture just as well as I. The Church knows it. The world knows it. What has the Church to say about it? In one tone or another she and her members are saying on every side of us that if this lukewarm, unenthusiastic, slipshod piety, which is so common, is not the best that we could desire, it is the best which in the present state of things, and for the large majority of men, is possible. "Just think," so seems to me to run the question of our self-excuse—"Just think what this age is, so rational, so business-like; just think what England is, what America is, so self-respectful, so reasonable, so self-contained; just think what we are, so prudent, so self-conscious, so unemotional. Can you conceive of us all afire as some commoner souls in ruder ages have been with the love of God? Can you imagine us praying aloud? Can you think of these streets of ours, or even of these churches of ours, ringing with the psalms of men who have forgotten whether other men are listening or not while they pour out the pent-up emotion of redeemed and grateful souls. Is it conceivable that with divine impatience this prudent people should come crowding like some passionate converts of old in other lands begging for the chance to give their riches for the conversion of the world to Christ?" Is not this what we hear from the silent lips of our repressed and moderate Christianity, my friends? To put it plainly, is there not a quiet assumption pressing down upon all of us, that in England and America in the nineteenth century Christ's ideal of Christian life is not a possibility? Oh, the great dreadful weight of that assumption! How our hearts and our hopes and our love and our joy are all crowded down and crushed beneath its weight! How it haunts the prayers we pray, the psalms we sing, the sermons we preach, the poor attempts at self-sacrificing help of fellow-man which we make! What can lift off the heavy load? Nothing but a going forth out of our own narrow idea of our possibility into God's great idea, into Christ's great idea. What a refreshment and freedom there comes when we go out there and know that not one of our assumptions has a moment's tolerance in the mind of our Great Master. He sees these modern towns of ours as truly able to be cities of God as was Jerusalem upon Mount Zion. He sees our life as capable of being filled with eager, ardent, self-sacrificing, self-forgetful piety as the life of any poetic people in any romantic age. Different, of course, our piety must be. A city of God unlike any other city where He has been enthroned, as every city in His realm must be unlike every other, but thoroughly His; not our own, but bought with a price, and living only for Him who bought us, so the Lord and Saviour of us all sees this hard modern life of ours. Not till we see it with His eyes shall we cast off the weight which lies upon us, and by our consecrated lives help the religion of our time and of our land to be what He, our Lord and Saviour, sees it capable of being.

The greatest of all applications of our truth, however, is to the personal life. There most of all a man needs the enlargement which comes of always feeling the infinite knowledge of God encompassing his ignorance. How easily with our self-distrust and spiritual laziness we shut down iron curtains about ourselves and limit our own possibilities. And this is truest in religious things. There are hundreds of people in this house now hearing me who have, with more or less deliberateness, said to themselves that, however it might be with other men, they never could be enthusiastic Christians. You have looked at yourself. You have seen how quick your perceptions are for the things of this world, how slow they are for the things that are unseen and everlasting. You have watched your own joy in self-reliance. You have seen what a proud man you are. You have observed the strangeness with which everything like an invitation to abandonment, to enthusiasm, to generous self-devotion comes to you; and you have said, "I never can be a Christian. I never can give up self-reliance, and in repentance and obedience and trust ask Christ to save me. I never can make another's will and not my will the law of my life. I never can call all men my brothers because they are Christ's. I cannot picture myself to myself upon my knees." Oh, what multitudes of men have said all that about themselves, and by and by, when Christ had claimed them and they were wholly His, have looked back and seen that it was the old life and not the new life which was strange; that the real wonder was how, with the privilege of prayer, they ever could have lived on prayerless for so many days and years! It would be terrible if, while you think and talk thus of yourself, God were not all the time seeing your larger possibilities. You cannot picture yourself to yourself upon your knees! When you say that, I seem to hear His voice replying to you : " If it be marvellous in your eyes, should it be also marvellous in mine? I know you better than you know yourself. You say you have not the power of religion, but I put it into you, and it is there. I never made a man without it ; and oh, my child, I made you. Among all my children capable of humility, capable of faith and tenderness and the sublime strength which comes out of gratitude to a Redeemer for redemption—among all my children capable of these, I did not make you like a stone. I can picture you praying, and when I see that picture I see your true self." It is the father crying out to the prodigal that his place is still kept for him at home. The moment that you believe God and let Him tell you what the true possibilities of your nature are, that moment you are free, and, believing on His word that you can be a Christian, the Christian life opens before you and your feet go in to its peace and strength.

It will not do for any one of us to make up his mind that he cannot be any good and noble thing until first he has asked himself what God thinks of him, whether it is as impossible in God's sight as it is in His. The moment a man asks that question the walls break down, the curtains are swept back. A broader hope, a larger treatment of ourselves begin. We dare to pray, not merely, "Lord, make me that which I know I ought to be," but, "Lord, make me that which Thou madest me for—that which Thou seest to be possible for me—and let me gladly take whatever larger possibility Thou shalt reveal." That prayer may we all have grace and faith enough to pray.

V.

IN THE LIGHT OF GOD.[1]

"In thy light we shall see light."—PSALM xxxvi. 9.

THE picture in the mind of him who wrote this psalm is very clear. Men are looking for light. With that insatiable passion which belongs to their humanity, they are running hither and thither seeking to know. And he who writes is in true sympathy with their search. To him too light seems the most precious thing on earth. Knowledge appears to him the treasure which is most worth possessing. But it seems to him that there is something which needs to be suggested to these searchers after light. They appear to him to be questioning this thing and that thing, as if the secret of its being, its power to be understood and comprehended, the light with which it ought to shine, were something which it carried in itself. He sees things differently. To him everything is

---

[1] Preached in St. Margaret's Church, Westminster, Sunday morning, 3d June 1883.

comprehensible and capable of being understood only as it exists within the great enfolding presence of God. To him it is only in their relations to the perfect nature that all other natures can become intelligible. He does not question the flower for its colour, or the mountain for its majestic form, or the river for its sparkling movement, as if each of them by its own action could clothe itself with light and shine out of the darkness, a clear and independent spot of glory. He looks up and waits and prays for sunrise. He expects the element in which alone the mountain and the flower and the river can display themselves. When the sun shall have risen and the sunlight shall be bathing everything, then everything shall glow with its own radiance; then he can study everything and understand it in its true element. Until that element is formed around all things, there is darkness everywhere. Is not this his meaning as he stands in the midst of the light-seekers and looks up to God and cries, as if in commentary on their eager searchings, "In thy light we shall see light."

The truth which these words thus include is one which we are constantly meeting, and which finds its illustrations everywhere. It is the truth that only within the elements where they belong, only as they are held inside the atmosphere of larger natures to which they bear essential and sacred relationships, can the finest and truest natures of many things be understood. See what are a few of the familiar illustrations of this truth. Have you not each of you some friend who, dull and dry by himself, becomes fresh and sparkling in the presence and under the influence of some other friend? That other friend is his element. When you are going to meet your dull companion you go and seek out first his elemental friend, and say to him, "Come with me, for I cannot know or understand this man except when you are there. In your light I shall see his light."

So the man toiling at his business has for his element the love for wife and child who live at home, and whom he loves. Looked at apart from them his life is dreary, and each act of his daily toil is dull and heavy as a stone. Looked at in the light of his love for them, every detail of his dusty energy glows like a star.

Or to take a wholly different illustration: a purpose of study, a great conception of what study is for, a true valuing of truth either for its own pure worth or for its noble uses, is the element within which the drudgery of learning, which otherwise would be all dark and dreary, shines with illuminations which make us its willing slaves.

So the prevailing moods and tempers of our

lives hold within themselves the specific actions of our lives, and give them their significance and worth. So every public deed, every turn of public policy, every action of our public men, exists within the enfolding atmosphere of the genius of our nation, and is to be appreciated and discriminated, is to be distinguished from the quite different thing which such an act or policy would be in Turkey or in France, only by an understanding of the national genius or nature within which it takes place. So the general's character and skill make up the element within which the soldier's bravery and labour live. Only by knowing the general's plan of the campaign can you tell what the soldier's hard work means. So the accepted doctrine, if it be really and spiritually accepted, gives colour to the acts which it inspires. Faith is the element of works. So what we think of man decrees what we shall think of men. The illustrations would be endless. Everywhere there is this enfoldment of the little by the great. Everywhere it is in the light of the elemental life that the life which lives within it and is its special utterance can be understood. Everywhere the act in its true element grows live and buoyant as the log grows buoyant in the water where it swims.

Do there not occur at once two earnest and

important warnings here, which we may well notice as we pass? If this be true, then you and I have no right to judge any life until we have called upon the element in which it lives to come and shed its light upon it. Not by itself, but as part of some great purpose, as the utterance of some intention, as the expression of some general character, so we must estimate and value every act, and all the active part of any fellow-creature's life.

And for ourselves, in our own lives, surely it is good that we should be conscious of and value the larger regions within which our specific actions are comprised, and from which they get their meaning. To be aware of purposes and allegiances which bind us, which make our lives great units, which hold us to the universe of things, thus to feel the pressure and the inspiration of our element about us, this surely is the secret of the best success and happiness of life.

I have dwelt thus long upon these first definitions, because it seemed to me as if in them there were the key to the experience of David, which he utters in my text, and of which I wish to speak to you this morning. He saw the world all full of seekers after light; he was a seeker after light himself. What he had discovered, and what he wanted to tell men, was, that the first step in a hopeful search after light must be for a man to put himself into the element of light, which was God. The first thing for any man to do who wanted knowledge was to put himself under God, to make himself God's man ; because both he who wanted to know and that which he wanted to know had God for their true element, and were their best and did their best only as they lived in Him.

If David's discovery was true, it was a great discovery ; it was a discovery which could never lose its value. It is just as precious for the students of this knowledge-seeking age, for the students assembling in our universities to-day, as it was for him back in the infancy of science, among the crude fantastic schools of old Jerusalem. But I beg you to think, also, what a noble and inspiring thought it gives us also about God! Too often have the minds both of religious and of irreligious men conceived of God as the great hinderer of human knowledge. Even those men who thought they honoured Him supremely have talked about Him as if He loved the darkness ; they have dwelt upon mystery as if it were something which God treasured, and which His children were to treasure for itself, as if they did not wish it cleared up and made light. They have imagined Him almost standing guard over whole regions of knowledge and forbidding them to the impatient intellect of man. That is not the idea of David; that is not the idea of the Bible anywhere. Against all the folly of the Church, and all the ignorance of unbelief which declares that God is darkness, stands up the protest of John, who cries, " God is light, and in him is no darkness at all;" and the glowing ascription of the light-loving David, who declares, " In thy light, O Lord, we shall see light."

I have talked of light as if it were identical with knowledge; and yet I am sure that the words make somewhat different impressions on you, and you will understand that they are not entirely identical. At any rate, you will understand that light means knowledge only when knowledge is most largely and deeply conceived. There is a knowledge which is not light but darkness, just as there is a lustre on the surface of the ocean which keeps you from seeing down into the ocean's depths. There is a superficial knowledge of the things to which men give their study—of nature, of history, of literature, of man—which, while it is wonderfully accurate in the facts which it recites, does not help to reveal, but glosses over and shuts away from our intelligence the depths and the essential glories of the things to which those facts relate. To such a sort of knowledge all laborious and minute study is always liable; but such a sort of knowledge is not light but darkness. When

David says, then, and when we say after him, that it is only in God's light that any man can see light, he does not mean, we do not mean, to say that the accumulation of facts and the thorough study of the surfaces of things may not go on in the most godless atmosphere and under the most blasphemous of students. What he does mean to say, and what the experience of man has borne its constant testimony to, is this, that the profoundest knowledge, the appreciation of the real meaning and radiancy of things—that this, which alone is really light, comes to man only within the light of God. I want to remind you of three or four facts concerning human knowledge which seem to me to give their confirmation to the doctrine of the old Hebrew singer's song.

1. First of all stands the constant sense of the essential unity of knowledge. Men study many things. Each man finds for a time contentment in his special science in the mastery of his peculiar facts; but as each man goes deeper into the knowledge of the chosen subject of his study, he becomes aware of how impossible it is for him to know that subject well, unless he knows far more than that. The student of the history of man finds that this wonderful theatre of the earth, upon whose surface the long drama of human history has been played, demands that it too must be understood before

the fortunes of the man whose life has been lived upon its stage can be properly valued. The study of the human body and the human mind are incomplete, each of them without the other. Each branch of natural science is twisted and twined in with all the rest. The most transcendent art has the roots of its methods in the human frame, and in the material of the earth itself. Everywhere this is the issue of man's study as he goes on farther and wider in any department; the conviction that no art or knowledge stands alone, that each is bound up in a whole with all the rest, and that to study any art or any branch of knowledge in entire independence of all others, is to come not to light but to darkness—to misconceptions of the true nature of things, and of the best conduct of life. All truth makes one great whole; and no student of truth rightly masters his own special study unless he at least constantly remembers that it is only one part of the vast unity of knowledge, one strain in the universal music, one ray in the complete and perfect light.

2. A second fact with regard to human knowledge is its need of inspiration and elevation from some pure and spiritual purpose. It is a fact which is assured by all the testimony of man's experience of study, that, not upon the lower grounds of economy and the usefulness of knowledge to

man's physical and social wants, but by some sense of a preciousness inherent in itself, of a fitness between it and the nature of man, of a glory in seeking it and a delight in finding it for its own pure sake, that only so have all the great revelations of truth come to mankind. The lower motives come in, no doubt, to lend their aid. The student finds a pleasure in the thought that his discovery, if he can accomplish it, will make him and his brethren safer and more comfortable in their daily life; but the most patient search and the most enthusiastic seizure of knowledge does not come from those motives alone. The knowledge which is sought as light must be sought with an enthusiasm which gets its fire from the pure value of the knowledge for its own pure sake. If among the young men who in our various colleges are pursuing their higher education there are any who are destined genuinely to enlarge the bounds of human knowledge, and to be recognised as light-givers by their fellow-men, this we are sure of concerning them, that they are among those who know something of the true passion of knowledge; they are of those to whom the opening doors of study bring exaltation and enthusiasm and delight; for it is only to such that light is given, and so it is only such that can give light to their fellow-men.

3. I think that another characteristic of the

best search after wisdom is the way in which it awakens the sense of obedience. I will not attempt to explain its meaning, but no man who thinks carefully and wisely will fancy that he has adequately explained it when he has attributed to mere superstition that sense which is always reappearing in the thought of man, that the knowledge which is highest in its nature and which it is most necessary for man to have, always comes to man by revelation, and can be attained only by the learning man's obedience to the revealing power. Very vaguely, very impersonally often, this idea has been conceived and stated. Sometimes it has seemed to mean no more than that man, in order to understand Nature, must be in sympathy with her and watch her ways instead of forcing her action into his ways. At other times it has taken sharp, crude, intense shapes like those which it has assumed when man, abandoning all use of his own powers, has seemed to think that there was nothing for him to do but to stand listening before a smoky oracle, or to peer into the entrails of slain birds in order to know the truth. But still, however vaguely or however crudely it has shown itself, the fact is very certain that man, when he has been moved most earnestly to seek for truth, has always thought of himself and talked of himself as of one who must be obedient to something, somebody, some power who held the truth which he desired, and who either would give it or could give it only to the obedient heart. In other words, all of man's loftiest search for knowledge has always seemed to be aware, not merely of two parties to the great transaction, but also of a third—not merely of a knowledge to be sought and of a man to win it, but also of a knowledge-giver, who was to stand between the treasure and the needy human life, and give to the obedient humanity the boon it sought.

4. Closely allied to this fact is the other one which yet remains to be mentioned with regard to the search of man after knowledge, which is the constant tendency which it has always shown to connect itself with moral character. It is easy enough to say that the whole affair of knowledge-seeking is a question of the intellect—easy enough to say that a clever libertine or a bright drunkard can learn and teach the facts of science or of history as perfectly as if his life were pure and sober ; but yet the fact is clear that mankind in all ages has tended to believe that moral purity and uprightness were genuine and necessary elements in the most perfect insight even into the problems of the world's construction or of the history of man, —that, at any rate, however mere facts might be learned by any acute and patient observer, the

meanings of those facts, the soul and inner substance of the things they studied, could only come to men who loved the right and tried to do it, and kept their hearts pure, unselfish, and serene with truth. All the old initiations to the mysteries of knowledge bore witness to this instinct. The man to whom the deepest known secrets of things were to be opened to-morrow must be purified to-night by lustrations that should signify his inner baptism. I do not ask now what was the philosophy which, more or less consciously, underlay this demand. I cannot doubt that it was some sort of assertion of the essential and inviolable unity of our human life, some sort of protest against the separation of the intellectual and moral life in man, as if such a separation made us two men and not one. What I want now to notice is merely the fact, the abundantly witnessed fact, that man in all times has had this feeling about the highest and completest knowledge, that one of its necessary conditions was morality, that only the pure in heart could see the fullest light.

See, then, what we have reached. These four conditions belong everywhere and always to the true light-seeker—the sense of the unity of knowledge, the perception of the preciousness and glory of knowledge for its own pure sake, the consciousness of discipleship and loyalty, and the persuasion of the need of moral fitness for the highest insight. In various proportions, in all degrees of clearness or of cloudiness, these are the convictions which have always filled the minds and inspired the souls of the seekers after light all through the world, all through the ages. The Hindu dreamer waiting for his vision, the young Jew at the footstool of his rabbi, the Greek listening for his oracle, the monk over his manuscript, the modern investigator of Nature and her wondrousness, the college student in his classroom—is it not true that all of them are men of light and not of darkness just in proportion as they keep alive and precious these profound persuasions, the unity of truth, the preciousness and dignity of truth, the need of obedience, and the sacred worth of purity. To him who lives in all of these persuasions, holding them all not merely as proved propositions, but as making together the element in which all his thought and study lives; to him everything grows luminous and opens its heart, and in the light of these, his four convictions, he sees the light of all the things with which he deals.

And what then? Is there no one conception in which these four convictions all unite, and in whose embrace they become not scattered discoveries or results of various experience, but parts of one complete idea which needs and which harmonises them all. If it be true that in the thought of God most simply and broadly apprehended—in the thought, that is, of a great, strong, loving Father, who knows all truth, and loves all men, and feeds men with truth as a father feeds his children with bread, making them with each new food fit for a richer food which He has still to give them—these four conceptions find their meeting-place; if as the young light-seeker goes with these four convictions working together in his soul they almost necessarily seek one another and unite into what is at first the dream, and by and by becomes the faith of a personal presence, lofty, divine, loving, and wise ; if this is true, have we not reached as the result of all this long analysis something like that which David puts with such majestic simplicity in his glowing verse. The combination of these consciousnesses makes, almost of necessity, the consciousness of God. As they are necessary to the search for light, so is the God in whom they meet the true inspirer and helper of the eternal search. You see how great the doctrine is. It is no low and unintelligible and incredible pretension, claiming that only to the holders of certain special doctrines can the truths of science or of history be made known. It is the lofty assertion of the divinest necessity of the human soul, that only under the care and guidance of the God in whom abide the unity and preciousness of truth, and whose pure-hearted disciple and obedient servant man, the searcher for light, can be,—in and under Him alone can the great fulness of truth be known or understood.

I have tried thus to analyse the causes which underlie the necessity of man for God in the search after the truest knowledge with regard to the earth he lives in, or the history of man, or his own nature. But, after all, in every such necessity there is much that entirely eludes analysis, and is recognisable only by the consciousness. It is in what we must always recur to as the filial consciousness, the sense of childhood, that man's perception of God always takes its clearest shapes. And when I try to describe to myself this thought of David about man's seeing all light in the light of God, no picture like the picture of a true and docile childhood seems to me to express it. A child in his father's house learns everything within the intelligence and character of his father, who has provided all things there, and is perpetually throwing light upon their proper use. Everything has its own qualities, but those qualities are made distinct and vivid to the child by their relation to the master of the house. Not purely in themselves but in his father's use of them and in their relationship to him does the child come to know the tools of the workshop, the furniture of the parlour, and all the apparatus of domestic life. So, I believe, it is with the child's knowledge of the larger house, the world-house, of which God is the Father. The young clerk in the counting-house, the young sailor on the seas, the young student at his books, the young mechanic at his bench, each of them finds the things which make his world shine forth with new clearness and with new glory, if he dares to think of himself as God's child, and of these things with which he has to do as the furniture of his Father's house and the means for the doing of his Father's will. No channel of direct investigation is closed up. Still the dictionary must be questioned for the language, and the market studied for the laws of trade, and the rock inquired of by the hammer and the microscope, and the sky and winds and ocean scanned with watchful eye; but over and around and through and through the whole process of inquiry, giving it dignity, hopefulness, dearness, and meaning, is thrown the pervading consciousness that it is always the child inquiring of the Father's things, and with the Father's watchfulness and care and love behind him.

Look at the life of Jesus Christ and you will see exactly what I mean. He knew the streets of Jerusalem and the lanes of Galilee and the history of His mysterious Hebrew people, and the hearts of the lilies and the souls of men; but He knew them all differently from the way in which the Hebrew scribes and scholars knew them. To Him they were all full of light. There is no other description of His knowledge that can tell its special and peculiar character like that. It was all full of light. And the other peculiarity of it was just as clear. It was full also of God. He knew everything as God's child in God's house. The history of the prophets and the heart of the lily both meant something about His Father. These two peculiarities belonged together. The world was full of light to Him because it was full of God. It was God's light in which He saw the deeper light in everything.

Just think of this, just think of how, this being true of Jesus, the more He saw of all the world, the more His Father's light must have become real to him, and then consider if there is not here the key to that difficult question, which perplexes us all, the question of how we can keep from outgrowing our religion as we grow up from childhood into manhood, and the world grows more complicated around us. The child is full of reverent and happy faith. God is to him everywhere. He prays as naturally as he talks. He

worships as spontaneously as he sings. But by
and by he is a child no longer. The silver gates
are open and the whole world lies beyond. The
elaborate manifold delightful life of manhood
takes him in. A thousand things to know, a
thousand things to do invite him. The simplicity
of life is broken into most bewildering multiplicity.
Then is the time when the boy's faith almost
always halts and is puzzled, when very often it
falters and falls. What can preserve it? What
can carry it safely through that first perplexing
acquaintance with the immensity and variety of
life and art and science, and bring it out a broader
and a stronger faith beyond? Nothing, surely,
except a demonstration by his faith of its capacity to comprehend and make its own all this
bewilderingly various life. Let the boy just
coming to be a man discern that the God in whom
he has believed in his small boyish way is the real
element by which, in which stars shine, states
grow, and all the complicated life of men goes on,
and must he not then grasp his faith anew as he
goes on to greater things and the larger relationships which are awaiting him? Let the growing
youth, as he passes through the door into the
new world, see the candle which he carries, and
which he is just about to throw away because he
thinks its work is done with the lighting of his

nursery where he is to live no longer, gradually open and expand until it seems to be the sun which lightens everything, and without which nothing can be bright or beautiful, and then must he not grasp his candle the tighter as the fascinating richness of the world begins to display itself before him? There is no other hope. No man carries his robe with him through the river unless he believes that he shall need to wear it on the other side. No man really preserves his religion simply from the memory of how it used to help him. It must help him now. No man keeps his boy's faith unless it opens new greatness to him as he grows older, and shows him how his full-grown manhood, like his earliest childhood, cannot do without it.

Picture Jesus of Nazareth set down in Rome with all the flashing splendour of imperial power all around him; or in Athens, with the wisdom of the philosophers on every side. Would the young Jew have cast his faith away? Too real for him the visions that had come to him in Nazareth! Too real for him the glory of His Father, which had filled His Father's house! He would have laid fresh hold upon that truth and love which he had never so needed until now. He would have stood undazzled in the Roman glory, unpuzzled in the Grecian wisdom, because he would have known that in his heart he carried the light by which they should give light to him. It would have been like David calmly saying in the presence of the terrors of Goliath, "The Lord that delivered me out of the paw of the lion and out of the paw of the bear, he will deliver me out of the hand of this Philistine."

There are men whose faith thus goes with them and becomes the power of inspiration for everything they do. Everything else shines with the light and works with the strength of their religion. I hope that many of you have read the interesting book which gives an account of the *Personal Life of David Livingstone*. It is a noble record of a noble history. But the great beauty of his life as it comes out there is in the centralness of his religion. Two of the greatest interests of the human mind and soul were always with him—science and philanthropy. He opened the desert and traced the mysterious rivers, and watched the wanderings of the stars. He trampled out the slave trade in whole regions of its worst brutality; but, at the heart of them, the man's science and philanthropy both got their light from his religion. He was first, last, and always and above all things the Christian and the Christian Missionary, carrying the glorious Gospel of the grace of God to the most miserably benighted of His children. He refuses to be called the mere scientist or the mere philanthropist. In the light of God he sees light, and he makes light in the mystery and sin of the Dark Continent. Therefore his fame has among the scientists and the philanthropists its own peculiar beauty.

The knowledge of God lies behind everything, behind all knowledge, all skill, all life. That is the sum of the whole matter. The knowledge of God! And then there comes the great truth, which all religions have dimly felt, but which Christianity has made the very watchword of its life, the truth that it is only by the soul that God is really known; only by the experiences of the soul, only by penitence for sin, only by patient struggle after holiness, only by trust, by hope, by love does God make himself known to man. So may he give us all the grace to know Him more and more. There is an evidence of religion which may be written down in books and learned from books, and when it once is learned it is all mastered. That evidence is good; but there is another evidence of religion which is never mastered and exhausted. It grows and deepens for ever and for ever. As the man becomes more pure, more penitent, more sensitive to the least touch of sin, more passionately eager to be good, so does he grow for ever more and more sure of

God. And to him, thus growing ever surer of God, the world he lives in becomes clothed with an ever diviner light, and the pursuit of truth becomes more and more full for ever of enthusiasm and of hope.

Of heaven it is written that "the Lord God Almighty and the Lamb are the light thereof." I should be glad, indeed, if anything we have thought to-day could make us see that this part of heaven at least may be begun below ; that not merely the earth we live in but our own especial life—our work, our study, our profession, our daily toil—may live already in the light of God, and become earnest and dear and sacred because of the depth and richness of our love and consecration to Him and to His Son, who shows Him to us!

VI.

THE SUFFICIENT GRACE OF GOD.[1]

"And he said, My grace is sufficient for thee."— 2 COR. xii. 9.

THESE words were spoken to St. Paul but not to him alone. They came to St. Paul out of a mysterious vision. They have come to many and many a Christian out of the experiences of his daily life, which, as he looked at them in the light of God, have seemed to him to be more mysterious and impressive than any vision which could be set before the most astonished eyes. They have come as the total result of life, its spiritual issue and result, to thoughtful men who, tired and dissatisfied in the details of living, have asked themselves and asked God for some great comprehensive meaning of it all. To such men there has come down from God his explanation: "My grace is sufficient for thee." The meaning of life, of its happinesses and its sorrows, of its successes

[1] Preached at St. Mark's Church, Kennington, London, Sunday evening, 3d June 1883.

and its disappointments, is this, that man must be fastened close to God and live by the divine life not his own, by the divine life made his own through the close binding of the two together by faith and love.

I want to speak to you about this great Christian conception of human life to-night. And first of all, I want to ask you to remember what a need there is for any true life that it should have some general conception of itself within which all its special activities should move along and do their work. What the skin is to the human body, holding all the parts of the inner machinery compactly to their work ; what the simple constitution is to a highly-elaborated state, enveloping all its functions with a few great first principles which none of those functions must violate or transcend,—such to the manifold actions of a man is some great simple conception of what life is and what it means, surrounding all details, giving them unity, simplicity, effectiveness. The degree in which the life, living in its details, is immediately and consciously aware of its enveloping conception may vary very much indeed. Some of the lives around which it is folded most compactly, to which it is giving the noblest unity and effect, are almost unaware of it, and would have to stop and re-collect their consciousness before they could give you a clear statement of what was their enveloping idea of life. Often in children, often in the most child-like people, the conception is doing its work, holding the life together, even when it is most entirely unrecognised. The degree of consciousness may vary, but more and more the worth, the dignity, the beauty, the usefulness of human lives seem to depend on the existence of some surrounding purpose or idea which makes each life a unit and a force. Here is a man all quavering and scintillating and palpitating with brightness: every act he does, every word he says, shines with genius; but every act, every word, shines separate and alone; each is a single, separate point of electricity, shining the more brilliantly just because of its isolation. Here is another man of far less brilliancy, but of a clear and ever-present sense of what life means; his electricity does not sparkle at brilliant points, but it lives unseen and powerful through everything he does and is, like the electric presence which pervades a healthy human body. My friends, is it not wonderful how strongly we come to feel, how perfectly clear in us in course of time grows the conviction, that to the second man, not to the first, the world must look for good and constant power. Is it not wonderful with what ever-increasing certainty of instinct we ourselves, as life grows more serious and full of exigency, turn away from the first man and turn to the second in our need?

I have wanted to speak thus of the need of some great comprehensive conception of life, before I came to the special conception of it which is in the words which God spoke to St. Paul. "My grace is sufficient for thee," He declared. That man's life is to have abundant supply for all it needs, to be rich enough, safe enough, strong enough, and yet that all this abundance is not to come by or in itself, but is to be its portion, because the human life itself is part and parcel of the divine life, held closely and constantly upon the bosom of the life of God,—that is the great conception of humanity and its condition which these deep words involve. See how they must exclude these two ideas which are for ever haunting human souls,—the first, that there is no sufficiency for man; the second, that man carries his sufficiency within himself. How these two ideas rule together, dividing among themselves the hearts of men. The timid, tired, hopeless, discouraged men go about saying, "Human life a predestined failure: full of wants for which there is no supply, of questions for which there is no answer. So, whoever made him, wherever he has come from, here on the disappointing earth there is this everlastingly disappointed man." And then, among such men, close by their side, the brave self-confident, self-trustful men go about saying, "Man ought to be satisfied; man must be satisfied; nay, man is satisfied in himself. Let him but put forth all his powers and he shall supply all his own needs and answer all his own questions." And then, among these everlasting wailings and boastings, in the midst of this mingled self-pity and self-conceit, the voice of God comes down declaring, " Nay, both are wrong: you must be satisfied, but you must be satisfied in me; you must have sufficiency, but my grace must be sufficient for you."

I think, then, that you can see how in these words thus understood, in a conception of life like this there are two propositions which meet directly and directly contradict the two tendencies of human thought with which we are most familiar in these days of ours. You see what these two tendencies are. They are very familiar; they meet us everywhere; they are here in our Sunday evening church. One tendency is to despair of satisfaction; the other tendency is to discover satisfaction in man alone. As I go through the crowds which fill our crowded century I hear these two voices on every side of me. One voice says, " Alas, alas! we want to know, but there is no voice to speak to us and to enlighten our ignorance. We want to love, but every object of love on which we let our affection fasten fails us. We want to work, but there are no instruments and no materials fine enough to give embodiment to these dreams that are in us. Life is hopelessly insufficient for man." And then out of the same crowd the other voice cries out, " Hurrah, hurrah ! man is sufficient for himself ! See how he is finding the answers to his questions everywhere ; and when his questions prove unanswerable, see how he is continually finding out that his question is a delusion, that such a being as he is ought not to want to ask such questions, that there are no answers to such questions, at least none that it is conceivably possible or really desirable for him to know !" Were ever such despair of man and such triumph in man met before as are met now in these days of ours? Tell me, are not these really the two things that men are saying over to themselves about the problem of existence ? Is not the question of mankind's life, as we hear its ordinary statements, apparently settling down to this, whether it will be possible for man to live with a permanent conviction either that there is in the world about him no true correspondent and answer to the deeper parts of his nature, or else that his nature and the world have in themselves all that his deepest needs require ?

Remember, this is not a question merely of the time at large and its philosophies; it is not a problem which one sees rising like a dark cloud as he looks abroad over the puzzled schoolrooms and the busy workshops of his fellow-men. It is a problem which meets us all whenever our own personal life is deeply stirred. A great change comes in your life, something that rends your whole being down to the bottom as an earthquake opens the rock; your life is torn to its very depths; you can no longer live satisfied with the mere pleasant sight of the green grass and flowers which grow upon the surface; you must look down and see what there is in at the heart of things. And then—oh, my dear friends, do not full many of you know it?—to the human heart all torn, distressed, bewildered, there comes first of all this problem, What shall I do? Shall I make up my mind that there is no rest, no peace, no sufficient object for my trust—that my demand for them is an impertinence? or shall I make myself my own sufficient strength, and find my rest and peace and trust in cultivating and admiring my own life?

To such an alternative what can we say? To the first side of it I think that there can be no doubt what must be said. Man cannot rest in the settled conviction of insufficiency. There is a deep and everlasting and true conviction in man that he has no power or need in his nature for which there is not a correspondent and supply somewhere possibly within his reach. The power of adoring love, of which man is distinctly conscious, brings him assurance that there is a being worthy of such love. The power and need to trust implicitly will not be answered that there is no strength so strong that man may give to it implicit trust. The everlasting questions will everlastingly demand their answers and believe in the possibility of finding them till they are found. This is to me conclusive. I can conceive of man's dressing up almost any insufficient thing in the pretence of sufficiency and making believe to himself that he is satisfied; but that he should finally and absolutely come to the conclusion that he must content him in everlasting discontent, and cease to ask and cease to struggle out of pure despair, that is something which nothing that I have ever read or seen or felt of human nature gives me the power to believe.

And what, then, is the chance of the other side of the alternative, that man shall find humanity as he discerns it in himself and in his fellow-men sufficient for his powers and needs? There is only one thing which everlastingly makes that impossible, and that is the strange fact to which all the history of man bears witness, that man, though himself finite, demands infinity to deal with and to rest upon ; he claims to have relations with the infinite. That fact is borne testimony to by all the ages ; that fact is the perpetual witness of the consciousness in man's heart that he is the child of God. The child may be reminded every moment of his limitations and his youth, and yet he always mounts up to claim the largeness of his father's life for himself. And so man, the more you make him feel his finiteness, so much the more obstinately will he insist on his right to a potential possession of the infinite. The perpetual witness to this truth is one of the most interesting facts in human history. You never can rule lines around one region in the realm of knowledge and say to man, " Know that. That is the limit of what you possibly can know." The very demand is a challenge. He will rub out your lines ; he will break down your walls ; and, with what perhaps seems pure wilfulness, but what is really a conviction that there is no knowledge in the universe from which he is essentially and eternally shut out, he will choose the very things which you have told him he can never know to exercise his knowing faculty upon. What truly enthusiastically human man will tolerate the drawing of any line, however far away, outside of which he shall be bound to believe that human enterprise shall never go? Who will let any limit mark for him the certain boundary beyond which no yet more wonderful invention shall be devised, and no yet more beautiful miracle of art flower out of the rich ground of man's exhaustless fancy? What man ever truly loves and sets a limit, consciously and absolutely, to the loveliness of that which he is loving? The love that defines the limits of its idol's loveliness is not entire love; pure love lives in its power of idealising, and loves the infinite in the finite type to which it gives its homage. So everywhere there comes the testimony of this endless reach of man after the infinite, and of his inability to rest upon anything less. Who that with the best human ambition is seeking after character can fix himself a goal and say, " That is as pure, as good, as true as it is possible for me, a man, to be?" Who does not, must not see the distance stretching far away, past anything that even his imagination can define? There comes no real content to the seeker after goodness until, behind all the patterns which hold themselves up to him with pride and boasting in their practicalness, at last he hears the voice of the sublime impracticable standard far out beyond them all calling to him, " Be ye perfect as your Father in heaven is perfect." Then the finite has heard the voice of the infinite to which it belongs, to which it always will respond, and straightway it settles down to its endless journey and goes on content.

These are the views of human life which seem to me to show that it is absolutely impossible that man should finally reconcile himself either to despair or to self-satisfaction. It is in views like these that I find my assurance in such days of doubt about the nature and the destiny of man as these through which we are passing now. It seems to me to be absolutely certain that if there is in man a real essential belonging with God, if in a true and indestructible sense he is God's child, then the reaching of the child's soul after the Father's soul, of the human soul after the divine soul, must be a perpetual fact; it never can be stopped. Agnosticism, Nescience, Pessimism, Secularism must be all temporary phenomena; none of them can be the settled and permanent condition of the human soul if man is the child of God. If he is not, if there is no divine relationship in him, then one is ready to accept whatever comes; for who cares whether a beast that is but a beast dreams that he is an angel or with a bitter wisdom knows his beasthood. Superstition or despair will matter little in a man who has no God. No! I cannot picture man with a God quieting, stupefying his restless filial heart so that no throb or leap of it, no sudden access of filial consciousness shall ever take him by surprise as he lives in the perpetual presence of his Father's works and love. Some sudden turn of the world-child around some unexpected corner of the wondrous house will thrill the soul with its profoundest consciousness. If man is God's child, then man cannot permanently be atheistic. This poor man or that may be an atheist, perhaps; this child or that may disown or deny his father; but the world-child, man, to him the sense that he was not made for insufficiency and the sense that he is not sufficient for himself, these two together will always bring him back from his darkest and remotest wanderings, and set him where he will hear the voice which alone can completely and finally satisfy him saying, "My grace is sufficient for thee."

And now, if this is where the soul of man must rest, we want to turn and see most seriously what is the rest which man's soul will find here; what will it practically, actually be for a man when the secret and power of his life is that he is resting on the sufficiency of the grace of God? We may say various things about it; and the first and simplest and most important of them all is this, that the grace of God, on which a man relies, must be a perpetual element in which his life abides, and not an occasional assistant and supernumerary called in at special emergencies when it is needed. You see the difference. I say to one man, "Who is your sufficiency? On whom do you rely for help?" and his reply is, "God." Very confidently and earnestly comes his reply. "God," he declares. But when he answers "God," somehow it sounds to me exactly as if he thought that God was a man in the next house, or, if you please, the captain of a garrison in the castle on the hill—some one, some thing, which was at hand, and at his call when it was wanted. I say to another man, "What is your sufficiency? Whom do you trust in?" and he answers, "God;" and then it sounds to me as if the sunlight talked about the sun, as if the stream talked of the spring that fed it, as if the blood talked of the heart that gave it life and movement, as if the plant talked of the ground which it was rooted in, as if the mountain talked of the gravitation that lived in every particle of it and held it in its everlasting seat; nay, shall we not say what is the simplest and the truest thing? as if the child talked of his father whose life lived in every act of his protected life—in whom (what wondrous depth there is in those deep words!), "in whom he lived and moved and had his being."

Do you not see the difference? Take special instances. Here is our bewilderment about truth:

God, who knows everything, is our sufficiency in our own insufficiency, we say. But how? One doubter, when his hard question comes, says with a ready confidence, "I will go and ask God," and carries off his problem to the Bible, to the closet, as if he went to consult an oracle, and as if, when he had asked and got, or failed to get, an answer, he would leave the oracle off in the wood and come back to the town again, and live his worldly life there on his own resources until another question too hard for his poor wisdom should come up. I do not say that that is wholly bad; but surely there is something better. Another doubter meets his puzzling question; and the utterance of his sense of God's sufficiency is simply, "God knows the explanation and the answer. I do not know that God will tell me what the answer is. Perhaps He will, perhaps He will not; but He knows." The knowledge that is in the father —so close and constant and real is the identity of life between the two—the knowledge that is in the father is the child's knowledge, even though the child does not know the special things which the father knows. Not merely there is an open road from the child's ignorance to the father's wisdom; the child's ignorance lies close bosomed upon the father's wisdom, beats and throbs with its pulses, and lives with its life.

And so it is with regard to activity and efficiency as well as with regard to knowledge. One man says, "Here is a great work to be done; God will give me the strength to do it;" and so when it is done it looks to him most like, and he is most apt to call it, his work. Another man says, "Here is this work to be done; God shall do it, and if He will use me for any part of it, here I am. I shall rejoice as the tool rejoices in the artist's hand." When that work is finished, the workman looks with wonder at his own achievement, and cries, "What hath God wrought!"

Everywhere there is this difference. One sufferer cries, "Lord, make me strong;" another sufferer cries, "Lord, let me rest upon thy strength." Do you say they come to the same thing? Yes, if the doing of the task, the bearing of the pain, is everything. Yes, if the only object is that the ship may not founder and the back may not break; but if, beyond this, there is hope and purpose that the man who does the task or bears the load shall himself become Godlike in his doing or his suffering, then no mere deposit of the strength of God can do the work—only the ever-open union of his life with God's, which makes the two lives really one, so that the power that is in God is not made the man's by being transferred from God's to him, but is his because it is God's.

Always there are these two kinds of men. The picture that was seen ages ago in the valley of Elah, and which is written in the second book of Samuel, is always finding its repetition in the world. David and Goliath are perpetual: proud, self-reliant, self-sufficient strength, the big hard muscles, the tremendous bulk, the gigantic armour of the Philistine on the one side; and on the other the slight, weak Judean youth, with nothing but a sling and stone, with his memories of struggles in which he has had no strength but the strength of God, and has conquered, with no boast, nothing but a prayer upon his lips. These two figures, I say, are everywhere; they are confronting each other in every valley of Elah all over the world: the power of confident strength and the power of weakness reliant upon God. Goliath may thank his gods for his great muscles; it is a strength that has been handed over to him by them; but it is a strength which has been so completely handed over to him that he now thinks of it, boasts of it, uses it as his. David's strength lies back of him in God, and only flows down from God through him as his hand needs it for the twisting of the sling that is to hurl the stone.

Oh, how the multitude stand waiting round every valley of Elah where any David and Goliath meet! how the Philistines shout for the battle as they see their champion step forth! how the Israelites tremble and their hearts sink when they see how weak their shepherd-boy looks! how the Philistines turn and flee when their giant falls! how the Israelites first gaze astonished and then surround him with shoutings as David comes back with the head of the Philistine in his hands! and yet how the same scene is repeated over and over again for ever: the arrogance of the Philistines and the timidity of the Israelites wherever anew power confident in self meets weakness reliant upon God, in any broad field or obscure corner of the world.

It is sad to see even Christian men and times fall into the old delusion. The Christian Church —so reads its history to me—seems to have been far too often asking of God that He should put His power and His wisdom into her, and make it hers; far too seldom that He should draw her life so close to His that His wisdom and power, kept still in Himself, should be hers because it is His. The demand for an infallible Church, for a comprehensive and final statement of all that it is possible for man to know about God, for an authoritative oracle of religious truth—a demand which haunts not merely the hills of Rome, but even the broad open Protestant pastures of our own communion—the fictions of priestly authority

for forgiving sin, for putting grace into sacraments,
—what are all these but the everlasting craving
for a deposit of truth and power instead of a vital
union by love and obedience with Him in whom
truth and power eternally reside—the everlasting
wish to be a reservoir instead of a river? The
Church of Christ to-day upon the earth, neither in
her individual members nor in any aggregation of
her ignorance to make wisdom in any conceivable
council or synod, knows the absolute truth with
regard, let us say, to the future destiny of men
who in this life live wickedly and die rebels against
God. Does it seem to you as if it were a dreadful thing that Christ's Church should be in ignorance about such an important thing as that? Not
if you really know how near Christ's Church is to
the heart of Christ; not if you understand that
she is joined to Him as part of His own life, so
that His knowledge of what are the awful secrets
of the future is enough for her, and she may be
content with His assurance that, He being what she
knows Him to be, it must be a terrible thing, and
a thing whose consequences cannot die speedily or
easily, for any soul to grieve His heart, which is
infinite love, or to disobey His will, which is eternal righteousness. Our Lord's disciples asked Him
to promise them that they should sit on thrones,
and He turned them away and said, " Ye know not

what ye ask." But they asked Him to teach them to pray, and instantly His teaching came: "After this manner pray ye: Thy kingdom come; thy will be done. Give us this day our daily bread." He would do nothing that should enthrone their lives in what might for a moment seem to be self-sufficient power; He would do everything that should fasten their life to His Father's life, with the continual pressure of continual need. Oh, that the Church and the Christian might have learned from the old story of the Lord's treatment of those first disciples what kind of prayers He always loves to have them pray, and what kind He will always answer.

I find in all the life of Jesus the perfect illustration and elucidation of all I have been saying, of all that I want you to remember and take with you as the fruit of having listened to me this evening. Jesus never treated His life as if it were a temporary deposit of the divine life on the earth, cut off and independent of its source; he always treated it as if it lived by its association with the Father's life, on which it rested. "Of that day and hour knoweth not the Son, but the Father," He did not hesitate to say; and the Father's knowledge was enough for Him. "Now, O Father, glorify thou me," He cried. I dare not try to unravel the whole mystery, to adjust the whole theology; but this I cannot doubt as I read these infinite pages which are ever new, that Jesus was always full of the child-consciousness; He always kept his life open that the Father's life might flow through it. When he lay prostrate, tired out, broken down on the mountain or in the garden, it was not that He might re-collect His shattered strength and be Himself; it was that in the silence and the struggle the clogged communication might be broken clear, and God flow freely into Him again. "Not my will but thy will, O my Father;" that was the triumph of the garden. "My God, my God, why hast thou forsaken me?" that was the agony of the cross.

What Jesus wanted for Himself He wants for you and me who are His disciples. Not self-completeness. When He calls us to be His, He sees no day, even on to the end of eternity, in which, having trained our characters and developed our strength, he shall send us out as you dismiss in the morning from your door the traveller whom you have kept all night, and fed and strengthened and rescued from fatigue, and filled with self-respect. No such day is to come for ever. An everlasting childhood! A perpetual dependence! That is our calling. And with that calling in our minds how much that seemed mysterious grows plain to us. If He is moving our life up close to His, henceforth to be a part of His, so that motive, truth, standards, hopes, everything which is in Him shall freely flow from Him to us, what wonder is it if, in order that that union may be most complete, He has to break down the walls that we have built around ourselves, which would be separations between Him and us. The going down of the walls between our house and our friend's house would be music to us, for it would be making the two houses one. The going down of the walls between our life and our Lord's life, though it consisted of the failure of our dearest theories and the disappointment of our dearest plans, that too would be music to us if through the breach we saw the hope that henceforth our life was to be one with His life, and all His was to be ours too.

And how clear, with this truth before us, would appear the duty that we had to do, the help that we had to give to any brother's soul for which we cared. Not to make him believe our doctrine; but to bring him to our God. Not to answer all his hard questions; but to put him where he could see that the answer to them all is in God. Not to make him my convert, my disciple; but to persuade him to let Christ make him God's child. Oh, my dear friends, if that were what we were seeking concerning one another, friend seeking it for friend, father and mother seeking it for children; if that were what we were seeking, there would be richer harvests for the Lord!

Through all eternity that grace of God, that sufficient grace, shall flow into the open hearts of God's redeemed, making them strong and brave for all the vast works which they shall have to do for Him and for His kingdom. It seems as if it would be enough for this life, as if this life would be well spent, if, as the result of all of it, by many lessons, many trials, many failures, the soul whose strength is in entire dependence simply learned and carried, perfectly learned, with it across the river the lesson that the soul of man cannot live except in resting on the soul of God, and perpetually gathering into it supplies of His sufficient grace. That lesson may we learn in any way in which Christ sees good to teach it to us.

VII.

THE CHRISTIAN CITY.[1]

"*And there was great joy in that city.*"—ACTS viii. 8.

THE city was Samaria, and the great joy was the fruit of the first preaching of Christ there. The disciples had been scattered by persecution from Jerusalem; and one of them, Philip, had come down to the city which the Jews despised, and there he had told the people the truth which the Jews rejected. All around him was the misery and sin of a great city. He offered them Christ. He told them of Him who had come to relieve misery and forgive sin. As a symbol of the new life which he told them of, he touched some of their sick people, and their health came back to them: many that were taken with palsies and that were lame were healed; into many a house where there had been only darkness he brought light. The brightness ran along the streets. Not merely

[1] Preached in St. Paul's Cathedral, London, on the morning of Hospital Sunday, 10th June 1883.

a few scattered souls caught the new inspiration; it seemed to fill the air and flow through all the life of the whole town. And there was great joy in that city!

There is something clear and peculiar in this joy of a whole city over the new faith. We can all feel it when a thought or an emotion which has lingered in a few minds starts up and takes possession of a whole community. It is as when a quiver of flame which has lurked about one bit of wood at last gets real possession of the heap of fuel, and the whole fireplace is in a blaze. There came a time when Christianity, which had lived in scattered congregations and in the hearts of devout believers, at last seized on the prepared mind of the Roman Empire, and all Europe was full of Christianity. So it is something new, it is a phenomenon possessing its own interest and demanding its own study, when beyond Christian souls you have a Christian city—a whole community inspired with the feelings and acting under the motives of Christianity. It may or may not embody itself in laws or institutions; it may or may not be recognised in terms in the constitution or charter; that is of little consequence. But a city as well as an individual is capable of a Christian experience and character. It is more than an aggregate of the experience of the souls within it, as a chemical compound has qualities which did not appear in either of its constituents ; it is a real new being with qualities and powers of its own.

I should like to speak this morning of the Christian city, the city filled with the joy and regenerated by the power of Christ. The subject falls in with the purpose to which this morning is devoted : the hospital collection, the contribution of this whole Christian city to the sick and needy, a municipal act of Christian charity. That purpose implies a Christian city. No heathen city ever did such an act. It is the utterance in a broad and simple way of that true Christianity which, in spite of all the heathenism that is still among us, is yet the power of our corporate life, and runs in the veins of our community.

Christianity is primarily a personal force, and only secondarily does it deal with bodies of men, whether with churches or with states. That is a critically important truth. The souls of men must be converted ; and out of those converted souls the Christian Church or the Christian State must grow. It is fatal to Christianity to try to reverse that truth. To begin by making the structure of a Church or a State, and expect so to create personal character, is as if you began to build a forest from the top, making a wilderness of leaves and branches, and so expecting to strike downward into trunks and roots. This is the error of all merely ecclesiastical and political Christianity. But none the less is it true that when the right beginning has been rightly made, when souls have believed in Christ, and then a great multitude of personal believers, who have been fused together by the fire of their common faith, present before the world the unity of a Christian Church or a Christian nation, that new unity is a real unit, a genuine being with its own character and power.

I am not sure how intelligible this is. I am not sure that it is possible to state it so that it shall be clear to every mind. It needs some familiarity with the idea, some power of abstraction, perhaps something of a poetic power, to realise the true existence of a Church or a city as a being with its own capacities and responsibilities; but when it is once apprehended it is very real—it is no figure of speech. We see the Church possessed as a whole of qualities which she must gather, of course, from her parts, but which we can find in no one of her parts. She is more permanent, more wise, more trustworthy than the wisest and most trustworthy of the men who compose her membership. The city is a being dearer to us than any of the citizens who compose it. Many a man goes out to war and gives his life gladly for his country who would not have dreamed of giving it for any countryman. There are indeed some men who seem to be incapable of any such thought, who never can get beyond the individual. But the extent to which these ideas of what we may call the corporate personalities, such as the Church, the State, the City, have prevailed, and the depth to which they have influenced the feeling and action of mankind is a testimony that they are not imaginary but real. The Bible is full of them. The Old Testament deals with bodies of men supremely: Israel is more than any Israelite; Jerusalem is realer and dearer than any Jew. The New Testament reverts to the individual, who, as we said, must always be primarily conspicuous in Christianity; but it too advances towards its larger personality, and leaves the strong figure of the Christian Church and the brilliant architecture of the New Jerusalem burning upon its latest pages.

But leaving these general thoughts, let us come to our subject. What is a Christian city? Is such a thing possible? Is anything more to be expected than that here and there throughout a city men and women should be Christians, believing Christian truths, living Christian lives, and looking forward to ineffable rewards beyond the skies? Can we conceive of Christianity so pervading the life of a community that not merely the souls shall be Christian, but the city shall be Christian, distinctly different in its corporate life and action from a heathen city which knows nothing about Christ?

Christianity, then, or the change of man's life by Christ, has three different aspects in which it appears—three ways in which it makes its power known. It appears either as Truth, as Righteousness, or as Love. Every soul which is really redeemed by Christ will enter into new beliefs, higher ways of action, and deeper affections towards fellow-men. Belief, behaviour, and benevolence, these are the fields in which Christ works. By a change in these He changes the whole man. In every Christian Christianity will show its triple power. Each man made Christ's man will believe more truth and do more righteousness and overrun more with love than when he was his own selfish servant. There will be difference in different Christians. In one belief will be most prominent, in another integrity, in another benevolence, as the fruit of his conversion; but in all three will still be present a truer faith, a purer righteousness, and a more bounteous charity.

Now take these one by one, and ask if a city is not capable of them as well as an individual. Again I say, as I reminded you before, that they must exist primarily in individuals; all spiritual character must reside ultimately in single souls; but still I think that it is manifestly true that an aggregate of individuals may possess in its own peculiar way the spiritual character which the individual possesses, and a city, like a man, have and exhibit Christian faith and Christian righteousness and Christian love.

1. Look first at Faith. Perhaps this seems the hardest to establish. There was a time perhaps, we say, when cities had their beliefs. There was a time when no man could live comfortably in Rome without believing like the Pope, or in Geneva without believing like Calvin, or in England or New England without believing like the king or like the magistrates. Then it might seem perhaps as if each city had its faith; then every proclamation was based upon a creed. But see how that is altered now. A thousand different beliefs fight freely in our streets, and it is almost true that no man is the less a citizen for anything that he believes or disbelieves. When these old times come back then you may have a believing city, a city with a creed; but not till then; and these old times are never coming back. But this is surely somewhat shallow. This implies that the only exhibition of a faith must be in formal statement. It ignores for the city what we more and more accept for the individual, that the best sign that a man believes

anything is not his repetition of its formulas, but his impregnation with its spirit. It may have grown impossible, at least for the present, that cities should write confessions of faith in their charters, or even make the simplest acknowledgment of the most fundamental truths in the headings of their statutes or in the inscriptions on their coins ; but if it is possible—nay, if it is necessary —that the prevalence through all a city's life of a belief in God and Christ and the Holy Spirit should testify of itself by the creation of certain spiritual qualities in that city, recognisable in all its ways of living and government, then have we not the possibility of a believing city even without a written creed or a formal proclamation. Just look at this city where you live. This is a Christian city— a believing city. And why? how do we know it? It is not because an occasional document is solemnised with the name of God. It is not because a few verses of the Bible are read each morning in your public schools. It is because that spirit which has never been in the world save as the fruit of Christian faith prevails in and pervades your government and social life, the spirit of responsibility, of trust in man, and of hopefulness. These are the spiritual results of Christian believing : they are not found in heathenism. When Christianity enters into heathenism the new faith of a converted country is testified to by a pervading sense of responsibility, a more confident and cordial trust in man, and an expectant hopeful enterprise, which together make up that spirit of vigilant and serious liberty which belongs to the best civilisation and under which you live. This is the Christian faith of your community, showing in all your public actions. It has not come by accident. It has entered into you through the long belief of your fathers which you yourselves still keep in spite of all your scepticisms and disputes, the belief in a humanity, created by God, redeemed by Jesus Christ, inspired and pointed on to indefinite futures by a Holy Spirit.

If we doubt this, if we doubt whether a city can have and show a Christian faith, we have only to ask ourselves what would be the consequence if a heathen belief were prevalent everywhere among us. We have some men who disbelieve intensely and bitterly in every Christian doctrine. They disbelieve in God, in immortality, in anything like spiritual influence. They believe in no redemption of humanity opening the prospects of eternal life. To them man is an animal, God is a fiction, immortality is a dream. The spirit of these men we know: it is hopeless, cynical, despairing. If they are naturally sensual, they plunge into debauchery ; if they are naturally refined and fastidious, they stand aside and sneer at or superciliously pity the eager work and exuberant feeling of other men. Such men we know. Now fancy such men's faith made common ; fancy their disbelief spread like a pestilence through all the blood of your city. What would be the result ? Would it be merely that souls would be blighted and cursed ? Would not the city grow weak? Would not public confidence be smitten to the ground and enterprise be paralysed ? Would any generous work be done ? Could either popular government or an extended system of business credit still survive, since both are based on that trust of man in man which is at the bottom a Christian sentiment ? Would you not have killed enterprise when you had taken hopefulness away, and given the deathblow to public purity when you had destroyed responsibility ?

No, the city has its Christian faith. It believes in and is influenced by its belief in the great Christian truths. Its belief is far from perfect: it is all stained and broken with scepticism. That disbelief to which many of our educated men have brought themselves creeps down in ignorant and half-unconscious ways, and saps the strength out of the belief of the uneducated masses. But still the Christian faith is the true faith of our cities. It is vastly more strong than many of you who spend your life in a little circle of people with the affectation of doubts upon them are ready to believe. Every now and then comes a revival. Such scenes as we have witnessed in England and America are surely the most explicable, the most intelligible sights that it is possible to imagine. "What does it mean?" we say; "when all seemed quiet, and men seemed settling placidly down into unbelief and indifference, all of a sudden this great outbreak? People crowding by tens of thousands to hear some homely preacher, the city shaken with the storm of hymns, thousands confessing their sins and crying out for pardon?" Is it not clear enough what it means? Here many of the men to whom the people most looked up have been sending down to the uplooking people the barren gospel of their scepticism. They have taught them that there is no God whom they can know; they have bidden them not dream of immortality. These teachings have sunk into the people's heart; they have gone down there heavy and cold. But by and by they have pressed too terribly upon the spiritual consciousness; the sense of God, the certainty of immortality, has risen in rebellion; the great reaction comes; the wronged affections reassert themselves.

> "A warmth within the breast would melt
> The freezing reason's colder part,
> And like a man in wrath the heart
> Stood up and answer'd 'I have felt.'"

One must rejoice in such a healthy outburst. To complain of its extravagances or faults of taste is as if you complained of the tempest which cleared your city of the cholera because it shook your windows and stripped the leaves off your trees.

It is then possible for a city to have a Christian faith. The methods by which it may be perpetuated and kept pure are open to endless discussion. No doubt the city in which a Christian faith is liveliest stands the most in danger of ecclesiasticism on the one hand, and of dogmatic quarrelsomeness on the other; but about this one fact we are most clear, that a city may believe, and as a city may be blessed by its belief. It seems to open an appeal to any generous and public-spirited young man, to which he surely ought to listen. Not only for your own soul and its interests you ought to seek the truth, and not be satisfied till you believe something with a clear and certain faith. For the community in which you live, because these streams of public and social life which run so shallow need to be deepened with eternal interests, because your faith in God will help to make God a true inspiration to the city's life; therefore, in addition to all the motives that belong to you alone, therefore you ought not to be satisfied without believing. 'Seek for the truth and find it. Not for yourself alone, but for the men about you, for the city that you love. Remember the simple old parable in the book of Ecclesiastes: "There was a little city, and few men within it; and there came a great king against it, and besieged it, and built great bulwarks against it: now there was found in it a poor wise man, and he by his wisdom delivered the city. Then said I, Wisdom is better than strength." And wisdom in the Old Testament means what faith means in the New.

2. The second aspect under which Christianity presents itself is Righteousness. A man who is a Christian holds certain truth, and then he does certain goodness; there is a new moral character in his activities. We pass on to the question of this righteousness. Is it too something that can belong to this gathering of men which we call a city, or must it be confined wholly to individuals? In this aspect can there be such a thing as a Christian city? The answer is not difficult. Certainly every city has a moral character distinguishable from, however it may be made up of, the individual character of its inhabitants. This is seen in two ways. First, in the official acts which it must do, the acts of justice or injustice, of deceit or candour by which it appears as a person acting in its official unity among its sister cities. But even more its moral character appears in its capacity of influence, in the moral atmosphere which per-

vades it, and which exercises power on all who come within it. You send a child to live in some village of the South Sea Islands, some heathen brutal community where vice is in the very atmosphere, and he is certainly contaminated. What is it that contaminates him? Not this man's or that man's example, but the whole character of the city where he lives. The brutality is everywhere, in all its laws, its customs, its standards, its traditions. It is not merely in this or that cannibal group who hold their frightful revel in its streets; the streets themselves are steeped in it; the very houses reek with viciousness. You send him back to live in old Pompeii, where the abominations which modern times have uncovered and made the subject of cool archæological study were live things, the true expression of the heathen city's spirit, the outward and visible signs of her inward and spiritual grace. As he enters in you see his soul wither and grow spotted with corruption. It is a bad city, and its badness taints him. We know what we mean when we say that it is a bad city; it is not the badness of one man or another of which we are thinking; the city is a real true being in our thought—lustful and scornful and godless. Then bring your boy and put him here in Christian London. It is not only this or that Christian whom he meets. It is a

Christian goodness everywhere: in the just dealing of the streets, in the serene peace of the homes, in the accepted responsibilities and obligations of friends and neighbours, in the universal liberty, in the absence of cruelty, in the purity and decency, in the solemn laws and the courteous ceremonies,— everywhere there is the testimony of a city wherein dwelleth righteousness. So true is the character in the city itself that you might clear the streets of London of all their present population and pour into their places the inhabitants of the South Sea Island town or of old dissolute Pompeii, and though of course before long the new population would be too strong for the old city and give it their character, yet for a time the character of even the inanimate city, of the stone and brick, would assert its strength, and the wild savages and classic sensualists would be unconsciously refined or sobered as they went among the houses where years of Christian purity and uprightness had left their influence. What is it that has made the difference? It must be Christianity; it can be nothing else. It is Christ in the city—the Christ who has been here so many years. And when we think how imperfectly Christ has been welcomed and adopted here—how only to the outside of our life He has penetrated, then there opens before us a glorious vision of what the city might be in which

He should be totally received, where He should be wholly King.

We dwell on the iniquity of city life in modern times. Indeed there is enough of it. But it is not the riotous and boastful wickedness of heathen times. Men have at least seen clearly enough the Christian standard, the Christ, to be ashamed of what they are not willing to renounce, and hide in secret chambers the villainies which used to flaunt upon the public walls. It is one stage in every conversion of the converted city as of the converted man. The next stage is to cast away the wickedness of which one has become ashamed. Of cities in the first stage there are instances everywhere through Christendom. Of the second stage—of the city totally possessed by Christ and so casting all wickedness away, there is as yet no specimen upon the earth, only the glowing picture of the apocalyptic city, the New Jerusalem, of which Christ is the Sun and Light, and into which there can enter nothing that defileth, neither whatsoever worketh abomination nor maketh a lie; a city so full to the very gates of righteousness that it casts out sin as light casts out darkness. That sounds very visionary and far away; but consider that to bring about that city so different from your London you need only vastly more of the same power that has made your London so different from Pompeii. The Christian city is not all a dream. Already we have a city which has enough of Christ in it feebly to turn away from its gates some vices which once came freely in to the old cities. Very far off, but still in the same direction, we can see the city so completely filled with Christ that no sin can come in, nothing that defileth, neither whatsoever worketh abomination nor maketh a lie.

There is, then, such a thing as a city Christian in point of righteousness. That old Jewish conception of a holy city is not all a dream. Purity and truth may belong to a city as well as to a man. Again we come to a lofty ground of appeal. If you are pure and true, you who are privileged to make part of a great city, remember—oh, remember!—that your righteousness is not for yourself alone, nor for the few whom you immediately touch; it is for your city. I am speaking to business men, who, if they will be really Christians, may help to put a more Christian character into business life. I am speaking to women of society, who, if they will be really Christians, may make the social character of the town more Christ-like, more true, serious, lofty, pure and intelligent—less sordid, sensual, and ignorant. I am speaking to young men, on whom it rests to develop or to destroy for their city the character that their fathers gave her. If you fail, you Christian men and women, what chance is there for the city? Not for yourselves alone, not for your happiness alone, here or hereafter, but for the city of which you are proud; for her character, which will become the character of thousands who are gathered into her, who shall be born in her hereafter, is there not a new motive to be earnest and pure Christian men and women in the love of God, in the service of Christ, by the power of the Holy Ghost?

3. There are only a few moments left me in which to dwell upon the third development of Christianity, which is in Charity. Truth, righteousness, and love, we said; faith, hope, and charity, and the greatest of these is charity. When a man becomes a Christian, he believes right, and then he does right; and then he tries to help his fellow-men. That is the old highway of grace, trodden by the multitudes of Christian feet for ages. And now again the question comes, can a city too have Christian charity? Can it do good as the issue and utterance of its Christian character?

The Christian character of charity is very apt to elude us. If a Christian man gives alms to a poor friend, it is laid down to impulse; and if a Christian city provides for its own sick and needy and homeless, it is laid down to economy. In either case the connection of the charitable act with Christian faith is lost. But this is very shallow. You say it is all impulse when you give your money to the poor; but what is the impulse? Is there no Christianity in it? Is it uniform? Is your impulse the same as the savage's? Has Christianity done nothing to keep down the other impulse to harm, and to strengthen this impulse to help your brethren? And so you say the city's charity is all economy; her hospitals are merely expedients for saving so much available human life. But, tell me, who taught her this economy? who told the city that a human life was worth the saving? If the hospital has nothing to do with Christianity, but is a mere expedient of organisation, how is it that the most highly organised among un-Christian nations have had but the merest rudiments of hospitals? No! The charity of a city is a distinct testimony to one thing which has been wrought into the convictions of that city. That one thing is—the value of a man; and that conviction has come out of the Christian faith. The city may not know where it has come from, as very few of us trace our deepest convictions to their source; but they have none the less sprung out of that gospel which has proclaimed for eighteen hundred years that man is the child of God the Father, that he has been redeemed by God the Son, and that his body is the temple of the Holy

Ghost. A poor neglected creature drops in the crowded street; a horse strikes him, and the heavy waggon crushes him as he lies; or in the blazing summer sun he is smitten to the ground insensible. Instantly the city—not this pitying man or that, but the pitying city—stoops and gathers him up tenderly, and carries him to the hospital, which it has built. It lays him on the bed which it has spread for him; it summons the best skill to set the broken bone or soothe the fever; it watches by his sleep, feeds him with dainties, finds out the potent medicines, cares for him tenderly until he goes out strong, or until the weary frame finds rest in death. Is there no Christ there? Is not this a Christian charity? Is there no connection between that strange devotion, so impersonal yet so instinct with all the love of personality and the truth which is in the city's heart and soul, that that poor man, in virtue of his humanity, is the child of God, the fellow-heir with Christ of heaven. Once there was a city which, when Christ came to it, hated and scorned Him; it seized Him brutally, dragged Him before the judgment-seat, and crying "Crucify Him! crucify Him!" would not be satisfied till it had nailed Him on the cross and seen Him die in agony. To-day here is a city which, if Christ came to it in person, would go out and welcome Him, would call Him Lord and

Master, and hang upon His words and glory in the privilege of giving Him its best. In that first city there was no hospital: the poor sick man dropped and perished; the children's lives vanished, and no man even counted them; the wretched leper was cast out to die among the tombs. In this new city the hospitals stand thick for every kind of misery: the poor fall sick, and the city's great hand is under them. Is there no connection between the rejection of Christ and the rejection of His poor; between the acceptance of Christ and the reception of His suffering brethren? Has not the Christian city a right to hear the Saviour's words as if He spoke to her: "Inasmuch as thou hast done it to the least of these my brethren, thou hast done it unto Me"?

I know the perfunctory and heartless treatment with which occasionally the methods of our public charity disown the spirit to which it owes its birth; but that is rare, and still the fact of the Christian city's Christian charity remains. Who doubts that if the city were tenfold more Christian than she is, if Christian truth and Christian righteousness were tenfold more the inspiration and law of her life, the hospitals would be multiplied and enriched till it should be an impossibility for any sick man to be left unhelped. Deepen the city's Christianity and the city's charity must deepen and widen too. If we could imagine any poor, sick, weak man, still sick and weak, in the midst of the overrunning health of immortality, finding his way into the heavenly city of which we spoke, and sinking lame and exhausted on the pavement of the New Jerusalem, only think how the faith and righteousness of the celestial community must leap into charity, and the poor sufferer be borne to the banks of the river of the water of life, and tended in the softest chambers of the holy city, where God Himself shall wipe away all tears from their eyes, and where there shall be no more pain.

Truth, righteousness, and charity—I beg you, fellow-Christians, who are also citizens of London, to think of your goodly city as a being capable of all of these. Never fall into any low way of counting her a mere mass of houses or a mere machine of trade. Honour her and love her, and try to make her more and more worthy of your honour and your love by faithful, upright, charitable lives, which shall contribute to her truth and righteousness and love.

You know why I have spoken thus to-day. To-day your Christianity and charity clasp hands, and the mother knows and claims her child. Not by a mere appeal to feeling, but by asserting the reality and responsibility of a Christian city, I have tried to make you ready for the solemn and beautiful act of Hospital Sunday. The sick and suffering are all around us; their cries are in our ears. They are the children of our Father, the brethren of our brethren. To-day your Christian city owns their claim. We forget our differences, and try to do the duty in which we are all one. If you will do it as you can, there shall be great joy in this city; not only because many a poor sufferer will be relieved, but because you shall have borne witness that Christ is verily among you—that this is indeed a city of the living God.

VIII.

THE GREATNESS OF FAITH.[1]

"Then Jesus answered and said unto her, O woman, great is thy faith: be it unto thee even as thou wilt."—MATT. xv. 28.

THESE are evidently the words of one who is yielding, one who, after some reluctance, is giving way. If we knew nothing about their connection, if we merely heard them by themselves, we should seem to see a closed hand opening and letting go something which it had been holding fast. And such reluctance, as we well know, is of many kinds. One man withholds that which he might bestow because he wants to make his gift seem more valuable; another because he wants to bind the receiver more closely to himself; another because he thinks that what he has to give has not yet been sufficiently deserved or earned; another because he thinks it will not be used in the best way. When these considerations have been over-

[1] Preached at St. Michael's Church, Chester Square, London, Sunday afternoon, 10th June 1883.

come, then the closed hand opens, and the gift is given.

You remember the story from which the words are taken. Jesus has travelled outside of the regions of the Jews, and there has come to him a Canaanitish woman asking Him to cure her poor afflicted daughter. He has hesitated and remonstrated, but at last she overcomes Him with her urgency, and He yields to her, saying, "O woman, great is thy faith: be it unto thee even as thou wilt." It would be possible to give reasons, which no doubt would be true ones, for Christ's reluctance. Each one of those which I suggested might apply; but I cannot but think that the truest and simplest way to look at this beautiful story, which I wish to study with you this afternoon, is to consider it as a record of the spiritual necessities of Jesus. The idea which seems to me to be in it is this, that Jesus gave the woman what she wanted just as soon as it was possible for Him to give it; and that, just as soon as it was possible for Him to give it, in some true sense He had to give it, it was impossible for Him to refuse it any longer. He was not holding it, as it were, behind His back, watching her face to see when was the best moment to give it to her. He was telling her of a genuine impossibility when He said, "I am not sent but unto the lost sheep of the house of Israel." He could not give her what she wanted then; but when by her belief in Him she had crossed the line and become spiritually one of His people, then the impossibility was removed, and we may even say, I think, that He could not help helping her.

All through the record of mercies and the miracles of Jesus there runs a certain subtle tone which puzzles us. He who is so powerful and merciful gives us still a strange impression of holding His mercy and power under some strange conditions which limit and restrict their use. He who is so free is evidently bound by chains too fine for us to see. I need not remind you that there were some villages where He could do no mighty works because there He found no faith. "Whatsoever ye ask believing ye shall receive," He says, as if there were some other condition besides His own great love which must decide whether any special prayer should find its answer. When the needy men and women come to Him we find ourselves watching to see which of them He will relieve, and we are sure as we watch that it is not any mere whim of His which will decide; there is some law which binds Him with necessity. Surely everybody who has read the Gospel at all sympathetically has felt this. I seem to hear, as I read, the sound of a great sea of might and mercy shut in behind necessities which it cannot disobey ; I seem to hear it clamouring to escape and give itself away along long stretches of the wall which shuts it in ; and then I seem to see it bursting forth rejoicingly where some great gate is flung wide open and it may go forth unhindered to its work of blessing. So seems to me the story of the power and love of Jesus held fast under the conditions of the faith of men.

Christ is too truly man like us, and we are too truly man like Christ, for us not to have seen in our actions glimpses of the same necessity under which He acted. We too act for our fellow-men under the perpetual conditions of their faith. Who of us that has ever tried to help his brethren has not come to places where he can use both of those words of Jesus, where he can say sometimes, " I can do no work here because of this unbelief," and sometimes, " Great is thy faith : be it unto thee even as thou wilt." Some regions there are in which it seems as if every power of use and helpfulness that we ever possessed were gone, or at least for the time were walled up and buried ; other regions there are where, almost without our will, the best that is in us leaps to the gate and hurries out to help some need which has summoned it with a peculiar desire and capacity of being helped.

The subject of the verse, then, and that of which I wish to speak this afternoon is " The Power of

Faith over Jesus." We are always talking as if the highest natures and beings were the least subject to law. A great many good people seem to talk as if the world would be more splendid, clothed with a completer dignity, if it were not all bound by necessities which it cannot escape, if every star moved in the sky and every flower opened in the garden, not because it must, but because, by some extemporaneous whim, it chose to. And so men look to those whom they call their superiors, and think that their superiority and privilege consists in their escape from law. The labourer plods to his work early in the morning dusk and sees the rich man's curtains still undrawn, and says, " Oh, if I were only rich like him, and could do as I pleased." The boy takes his task at school, and dreams as he does it of the days when school shall be over and nobody shall any longer set him tasks. As we go on we find we are all wrong. The higher the nature the more imperative has grown the law. The rich man lying in his bed envies the labourer's easy whistle under his window. The merchant calls the schoolboy free. He who must do only what a few of his fellow-men, who are his special masters, can order him in formal commandment, and can enforce by stated penalties, has no conception of the perfect servantship of that life which has all men for its masters, and must obey any one of them, no matter who he be, who speaks to it with that entire openness and power to be helped which we call faith.

I beg you to observe how definite and clear an idea there is here of the way in which Christ gives His mercies to mankind. Evidently there is some inequality in the distribution of them. Any man can see that. Men have always seen it. Christ makes some men good and brave and holy; other men He seems to leave untouched. Some men He saves; other men He seems to leave unsaved. Men have always seen that, and they have always tried to explain it. They have tried the explanation of election, and they have tried the explanation of desert. They have said, "Christ chooses to save these and chooses to leave those unsaved." That explanation has not satisfied men; it has seemed too much to leave out man. Then they have said, " These men have deserved to be saved, and those men have not deserved it." That explanation also has seemed insufficient. It has seemed too much to leave out Christ, or to bring Him in only a sort of bookkeeper and paymaster of the moral world. But still this other explanation remains. Christ saves all whom He can save, all who are savable. Doing all that He can first to make men willing to receive Him, He then at last is in the power of their willingness. This surely is an intelligible idea of Christ and of the way in which He treats mankind ; this certainly lets us understand both of those words of His, which are but specimens of many other words that He said : " The Son of Man is come to seek and to save that which was lost," and " To as many as received Him gave He power to become the sons of God."

It will be good for us first to see, what I have already hinted, how widely prevalent the principle is which comes to its consummation in the giving of Himself by Christ to men. Everywhere faith, or the capacity of receiving, has a power to claim and command the thing which it needs. Nature would furnish us many an exhibition of the principle. You plant a healthy seed into the ground. The seed's health consists simply in this, that it has the power of true relations to the soil you plant it in. And how these spring-days bear us witness that the soil acknowledges this power : no sooner does it feel the seed than it replies ; it unlocks all its treasures of force ; the little hungry black kernel is its master. " O seed, great is thy faith," the ground seems to say ; " be it unto thee even as thou wilt ;" and so the miracle of growth begins. Or a human mind comes to an idea. What shall it be? Let us say the idea of cause and purpose running through and filling all creation. Clothe that idea in your imagination with consciousness ;

let it know what truth it carries in its heart; think of it as pondering to whom it shall deliver up that truth. There cannot any longer be a doubt when it has once found the mind that really sympathetically believes in it. It fills that mind with inspiration; it sends its force all through its action. Other minds touch it, and it gives them nothing. The man who in the most entire sympathy believes in the idea lives by it; all his movements become lofty, calm, fruitful with its influence. And so still more about a man. Why, it becomes a commonplace of all social life which is in the least thoughtful and observant, that no man gets anything out of a fellow-man unless in some degree, in some way, he believes in him. Here is a man whose life is full of business: his face, his hand, his name are everywhere; there is no movement in the community in which he does not take a part; there is no cause in which his aid is not invoked. What is that man to you, a fellow-citizen of his, before whose eyes he is for ever standing out in some new manifestation of his energy? Does not everything depend upon whether you personally believe in him? Suppose that you do not; suppose that all his tireless activity has only succeeded in impressing you with the conviction that he is a selfish, superficial busybody; suppose that, seeing how different his ways of working are from yours, or finding yourself at variance with him about something concerning which you feel perfectly sure that you are right, you have come to believe that he is insincere; suppose that some blunder of his has seemed to you to show such essential rottenness that you cannot trust anything about him? What then? That man's good, whatever good there may be in him, is shut up from you completely. He can do nothing for you; you can get nothing out of him. Some lessons, some suggestions from his life you may collect, but they will be to you only what they would have been if you had read them in a book or a newspaper. The man himself—not what he knows and says, but what he is—the man himself is as closely and tightly locked away from you as are the treasures in the bank's vaults from the poor vagrant who sleeps at night on the bank steps or paces up and down its sidewalk.

This is the reason why a disbelieving life becomes a barren life. You know how very common it has grown for men to think it a sign of wisdom and profound experience to distrust their fellow-men. The reason why one dreads to see a temper such as that increase is that the nature which distrusts gets nothing from the men in whom it disbelieves. One of the reasons why youth is the growing and accumulating period of life, the period in which harvests of truth and hope and character are gathered in, is that youth naturally and instinctively believes. By and by the man grows up, and then, distrusting his fellow-men, he walks over their hidden riches as the ignorant traveller walks over an unopened mine. Oh, my dear friends, young men and old, try to respect and trust just as far as you can the men with whom you most profoundly disagree, for so only can you get from them the peculiar riches which they have to give you. A staunch and settled Conservative, who is never going to be anything but a Conservative, if he respects the ability and honesty of some stout Radical, keeps open a channel through which something of what value there possibly may be in the Radical's Radicalism may flow into him. The Radical who honours a Conservative gets something of what value there may possibly be in his Conservatism. The more men you honour the more cisterns you have to draw from. Men of other parties, other Churches, other trades than your own, must acknowledge the demand which your faith makes on them, and give you whatever each of them may have worth the giving.

And if we stand not upon the side of the receiver but upon the side of the giver, the same truth is full of force. You want to give your intelligence, your thought, your wisdom, such as it is, to the little circle in which God has set you to live. It is not conceit that prompts you; it is a real desire to be useful. How necessary it is that at the very outset you should know our truth—that it is only to faith that such gifts can be given. Men and women are standing everywhere, all over the world, urging their advice and experience upon other people who do not believe in them. These other people have nothing against them; they do not hate them or despise them; but they have no faith in them. Faith is a positive thing, not merely negative. Not to disbelieve in a man is something very different from, very far short of, believing in him. Such men trying to enlighten and help other men who have no faith in them are like suns without atmospheres. No matter how bright they shine, the world which they want to enlighten gets no light from them. You must build the atmosphere before you can send down the light. You must win men's faith before you can do anything to make them wise or happy. Therefore it is that the mere amount of a man's intellectual power or the mere degree of truth in a man's doctrine is never a complete test or assurance of the power he will have over other men. A crazy chatterer or a blatant infidel will make the whole world listen and fill men with his folly if he can only make men believe in him; while

Wisdom herself may cry aloud in the chief place of concourse and no man hear, and the whole crowd go away as foolish as it came. If you really want to help your fellow-men, you must not merely have in you what would do them good if they should take it from you, but you must be such a man that they can take it from you. The snow must melt upon the mountain and come down in a spring torrent, before its richness can make the valley rich. And yet in every age there are cold, hard, unsympathetic wise men standing up aloof, like snow-banks on the hill-tops, conscious of the locked-up fertility in them, and wondering that their wisdom does not save the world.

I think that in such thoughts as these there comes out more clearly than any deliberate definition can embody it what is meant by faith. The best things in this world can be defined only by a description of their result. No man can tell me what the sunlight is except by what it does. The essence of life is utterly inexplicable; the action of life all men can see. And so of faith. Faith as I have talked of it to you to-day is such a relation of one being to another higher being as opens the higher being's nature to the lower, and makes a ready gift of the higher to the lower possible. "Ah, then," says the dogmatist, "I see that I was right. Faith is a proper understanding, a true idea, a correct creed. You must have that before the being higher than yourself can give himself to you." And then the sentimentalist cries, "No, I was right; faith must be feeling. Love and trust your superior, and he can help you." And yet another man, the moralist, says, "Was not I right? Is not faith simply obedience? Do your master's will, and he will put his nature into you." And as they all speak, anybody who has really got hold of the great truth sees how partial they all are, sees that faith is something greater than they each describe it, sees that it must include and must outgo them all: for I may know all the facts about a man, and yet his nature stand shut tight against me; and I may love and trust a man so foolishly and superficially and sillily, that he can do nothing for me; and I may follow a man's footsteps, and be in no more real communion with him than his dog. Sometimes all these unite, and something else, indefinable but absolutely recognisable, is added to them—something which comes in as additional to everything that can be defined in the substance of a friendship—and then, and not till then, the gates are opened and the lower nature becomes wise with the wisdom, strong with the strength, of the higher, lives by its life, judges with its judgment, knows with its knowledge. The power of that union, the complete and open resting of the life that depends on the life that supplies, that is faith.

In deep distress sometimes, sometimes in the most perfect and entire calmness, sometimes in the full current of most busy life, sometimes, as if it were the crown and sum of living, on the death-bed, when the snapping of old ties is like the cracking of the winter ice at the approach of spring-time,—at any time, in any place, wherever God wills, whenever the man's soul is ready, the gates open slowly or suddenly; the soul has faith in God; and God is given to the soul. The whole of life until that comes is but a growth, a struggle, a reaching-out to that. Life is but the mere shell of life until it comes. Life is faith. To believe in God is to be filled with Him, to enter into life eternal, and to have it enter into us.

But I must come back from what I hope has not seemed a wandering from the spiritual substance of my text to its words. Here was this woman whose faith had such a power over Jesus that He could not resist it. I hope that we have got some glimpse of what that means. The secret of it all to me is this—Jesus was the manifestation of God. God, with His power and love, was, so to speak, humanly manifest in Jesus. That human form, walking with self-witnessing evidence of divinity there among men, was not merely the declaration of God's love and power; it was God's love and power actually here. Now when this woman, by some such comprehensive action as I was just trying to describe, believed in Him, she was really claiming that in that human manifestation of God she in virtue of her humanity had a true part and might press a true claim. It is almost like this. It is almost as if a reservoir of water were established in a thirsty city for the city's use, and some citizen of that city came and said, "I have a right to some of it; give me my share." And his claim was allowed by the servant in whose charge the reservoir was placed; allowed, because he was one of those to whom the water belonged. So this woman said to Christ, "I in my human need have a right to you, who are the love of God humanly manifest." And Christ replied, "Indeed you have, and that claim of yours is itself the assurance of your right. No man can claim me so and not have me. Such a claim opens the channels between your life and mine, and what there is in me must flow into you." Something as real, as essential, as natural, as inevitable as that seems to me to be in His words when He says, "Great is thy faith: be it unto thee as thou wilt." When He said to His disciples these other deep words, "As the branch cannot bear fruit of itself except it abide in the vine, no more can ye except ye abide in Me," He really was teaching the same truth. There is a natural eternal relationship and openness between the life of man and the life of God. To have that openness closed is unbelief; to have that openness wide open is faith; and faith is health and life.

It is only with this truth, I think, that we can get and keep any true hold of the vast and bewildering idea of God's care for all His creatures, with all their small and separate lives. How hard it is for us to keep that truth, even while we feel that life would be worth very little to us if we did not have it. And what makes it so hard for us to hold appears to me to be the artificial conception which we have of the connection between God and His creatures. We talk about God's remembering us, as if it were a special effort, a laying hold by His great mind of something outside of Himself, which He determined to remember. But if we could only know how truly we belong to God, it would be different. God's remembrance of us is the natural claiming of our life by Him as true part of his own. When the spring comes, the oak-tree with its thousands upon thousands of leaves blossoms all over. The great heart of the oak-tree remembers every remotest tip of every farthest branch, and sends to each the message and the power of new life. And yet we do not think of the heart of the oak-tree as if it were burdened with such multitudinous remembrance, or as if it were any harder work for it to make a million leaves than it would be to make one. It is simply the thrill of the common life translated into these million forms. The great heart beats, and wherever the channels of a common life are standing open the rich blood flows, and out on every tip the green leaf springs. Somewhat in that way it seems to me that we may think of God's remembrance of His million children. In some hut to-day some poor sick sufferer is wearing the hours out in agony, longing for the evening as all last night he longed for the morning which seemed as if it would never come. Or in some obscure shop to-day some insignificant workman is doing some bit of faithful and useful but unnoticed work. You do not hesitate to speak to each of them and say, " God remembers you. He never forgets you for a moment." But how can you represent to your spiritual imagination, or, what is harder still, to theirs, the fact of that remembrance? It must be by the realisation of an open channel of continuous and common life between God and that patient sufferer, that toilsome worker. They are far-off leaves on the great tree of His life; far-off, and yet as near to the beating of His heart as any leaf on all the tree. He remembers them as the heart remembers the finger-tips to which it sends the blood. He gives them Himself because they are His in such profound reality that they are more than His, they are really He. If any doubt about Him, issuing from them, stops up the channel so that He cannot get to them, He waits behind the hindrance, behind the doubt, and tries to get it away, and feels the withering of the unbelieving, unfed leaf as if a true part of Himself were dying. And when the obstacle gives way, and the doubt is broken and the path is once more open, it is almost with a shout which we can hear that the life-blood leaps to its work again; and the sufferer wins new strength, and the worker wins new courage, by what it calls the renewed remembrance of God, but what is really the soul's renewed claim, which gives God once more the power to show His never-changed, ever unchangeable remembrance.

Through all that I have said to-day there runs one truth which I cannot state too simply and strongly, as my time draws near its close. I want to make you feel it and know it if I can. It is the necessary power that the weaker has over the stronger, the lower over the higher. It is a power which develops as all life grows higher, and which comes to its completeness when we get up into the region where man has to do with God. The lowest conditions of life hardly know it at all. Think of the masteries that are strongest and most imperative in two communities at the opposite extremes of social life. Into a village of savages comes some ruffian, more big and brutal than any other who is there, stronger in limb, bolder in arrogant courage; and all the savage village owns him as its master; all its people are at his feet in admiration and obedience; what he bids them they will do. Then turn to the other extreme. In some civilised village of England and America there is heard the cry of a suffering infant, the story of some wrong done to a little child comes to men's pitying ears, and all the village is stirred and will not rest until the wrong be righted, and the little child relieved. That little child with its woes is the master of those strong and busy men; his cry of pain summons them from their work as a bugle calls the soldiers to the field.

This power of weakness over strength comes to perfection in Jesus. Could there be a more complete picture of it than shines out in His own story of the shepherd and the sheep. The shepherd has folded his ninety-and-nine; everything is safe and strong and prosperous; he stands with his hand upon the sheepfold gate; and then, just as he seems all wrapped up in the satisfaction and completeness of the sight, there comes, so light that no ear except his can hear it, the cry of one poor lost sheep off in the mountains, and it summons him with an irresistible challenge, and his staff is in his hand instantly, and he turns his back on everything else to be the slave of that one lost sheep till it is found. What a wonderful and everlasting and universal story that parable is!

Oh, my dear friends, we have not entered into Christ's salvation, He has not rescued and redeemed us into His own divine life, until that which was true of Him is also true of us. Do we know as He knew this power of the weakest? Are our ears quick as His were to hear through every tumult the far-away cry of any poor human soul that needs us? Are our hearts quick as his was to own the right which that cry has to our instant attention and obedience? If they are not, our life is very poor. For we are fed through our obediences; and he who only knows what it is to obey those who are stronger than himself, he who has never felt the imperiousness of the need which cries up to him out of some depth of want or pain, has missed one-half, the largest and richest half, of the nourishment and enrichment which God provided for his human life.

We may dare to believe that in this service of weakness, this obedience to need, this submission of His power to the demands of His feeblest brethren, Christ our Lord found part of the development of His divine consciousness. Every beggar whom He met was a king to Him. Let us not think for a moment that that was something which belonged only to the days when He was here upon the earth. It is true still. When you and I are weak, Christ in a true sense owns the claim of our weakness and comes to serve us with His love. Behold, how this transfigures life! The times that make us weakest and that force our weakness most upon us, and make us most know how weak we are, those are our coronation times. The days of sickness, days of temptation, days of doubt, days of discouragement, days of bereavement and of the aching loneliness which comes when the strong voice is silent and the dear face is gone, these are the days when Christ sees most clear the crown of our need upon our foreheads, and comes to serve us with His love.

Faith is the king's knowledge of his own kingship. A weak man who has no faith in Christ is a king who does not know his own royalty. But the soul which in its need cries out and claims its need's dominion — the soul that dares to take the prerogative of its own feebleness and cry aloud, "Come to me, O Christ, for I need Thee," finds itself justified. Its bold and humble cry is honoured and answered instantly; instantly by its side the answer comes: "Great is thy faith: be it unto thee even as thou wilt. What wilt thou that I should do unto thee?"

IX.

"WHY COULD NOT WE CAST HIM OUT?"[1]

"Then came the disciples to Jesus apart, and said, Why could not we cast him out?"—MATTHEW xvii. 9.

MAN'S perpetual surprise at his own weakness is one of the most significant and pathetic sights in human history. Sometimes it seems as if the human race, always struggling with evils which it never overcomes, taking up in each new generation the unfinished fights with want and woe and sin and folly, often appearing to lose the ground which the old generations won, and slipping back to the bottom of the hill to begin the toilsome climb again—sometimes it seems as if man must accept failure as his fate, and frankly say, "I cannot do this which I have dreamed of doing. I was made too weak," and so abandon the attempt. But no! That time never comes with the race, and hardly ever with the individual. Sometimes

[1] Preached in Wells Cathedral, Sunday morning, 17th July 1883.

the wondering question loses its energy and dwindles into a weak querulousness. But still it continues to be asked ; still man, though prostrate on the ground, keeps sight of his ambitions ; still, though he lets himself grow weak and little, he wonders why he is not strong and great ; still, though he treasures in his heart the bad spirits of idleness and sensuality and selfishness and cruelty, something about him always bears witness that he knows they are intruders there ; still he goes about asking, "Why can I not cast them out?" never ceasing to be surprised at his own weakness and to seek for its explanation. It is the most significant and pathetic fact in all our history ; it shows how native and how persistent in man is his conviction of his essential greatness. The boy starts on his first conscious moral struggle as if it were a bit of play, the wrestling with an adversary who was just strong enough to give him the glow of exercise, but whom he was certain to cast down to the ground at last. By and by he looks up panting and puzzled, amazed to find that the struggle has apparently settled down into the law and habit of his life, and cries with half-exhausted breath, "Why cannot I cast him out?" Three score and ten years later the old man, with unabated hope but with unfinished struggle, steps down into the river through which he must go to reach the peace of God, and his last murmur is a repetition of the same old surprise, as he makes one last effort to throw his sin away—" Why cannot I cast him out?" And all the way between, the struggle has been going on, and man, always weak, has never ceased to be surprised at his own weakness. It is the most significant and most pathetic sight in his history.

The words belong, as you remember, to the story of what immediately followed Christ's transfiguration. The Lord comes down from the mountain on which he has been glorified and finds a poor lunatic boy in convulsions at the mountain's foot. His disciples are trying to cure the unhappy child. How we can see their helplessness! Their association with Jesus had taught them to believe that such affliction could be cured, but when they tried they could not do it. Still the poor boy raved on. At last, when they are ready to give up in despair, their Master comes in sight. The father of the child turns eagerly to Him; he tells Him how the disciples had failed; and then Jesus "rebuked the devil; and he departed out of him : and the child was cured from that very hour." Then it was that "the disciples came to Jesus apart, and said, Why could not we cast him out?" They could not accept their own failure. They must have an explanation of their weakness. And Jesus tells them that the reason of their failure is their unbelief. He says, "If you had had faith you could have done it. You were weak because you did not fill yourselves with the power which stood behind you. If you had faith you could remove mountains, and nothing could be impossible unto you."

In all this story I think there is a graphic parable of that truth concerning human life which I have tried to state. Man is surprised at his own weakness. He tries his strength and fails. How the whole history of humankind is like that scene which took place at the foot of Tabor while Jesus was being transfigured on the top. You remember how, in Raphael's great painting of Christ's Transfiguration, the whole story is depicted. Up above Christ is hovering in glory, lifted from earth and clothed in light and accompanied on each side by His saints. Down below, in the same picture, the father holds his frantic child, and the helpless disciples are gazing in despair at the struggles which their charms have wholly failed to touch. It is the peace of divine strength above; it is the tumult and dismay of human feebleness below. But what keeps the great picture from being a mere painted mockery is that the puzzled disciples in the foreground are pointing the distressed parents of the child up to the mountain where the form of Christ is seen. They have begun to get hold of the idea that what they could not do He could do. So they are on the way to the faith which He described to them when they came to Him with their perplexity.

Let the picture help to interpret them to us, and is not the meaning of Christ's words to His disciples this? He claims the disciples for Himself. He tells them that the reason of their failure is that they have been trying to do by themselves what they can only do when He is behind them, when their natures are so open that His strength can freely flow out through them. That, I think, is what He means by faith. Indeed, I think that there is hardly any word of Christ's in which the true spiritual nature of faith shines out so clearly. The man who is so open Christward that Christ is able to pour His strength out through him upon the tasks of life has faith in Christ. The man who is so closed Christward that nothing but his own strength gets utterance upon the tasks of life has not faith, and is weak because of his unbelief. That is really Christ's description of the interesting and pathetic sight of which I have spoken—of the undying wonder of man at his own weakness. This is the subject of which I wish to speak to you to-day and to make it plain to you if I can.

There are, then, two different ideas about the

way in which the problems of the world are to be solved and the salvation of the world, whatever it is, is to be brought about. Pure irreligion looks to man to do it. Let man go on thinking, inventing, planning, governing, and the result must come. Evil will be legislated or engineered out of the world, and all the better possibilities of man attained. Upon the other hand, a certain kind of religion looks to God to do it. Let man lie still, purely submissive, without a movement or a will, and God in His good time will bring the happy end. The first of these two ideas has no faith, and it fails. By and by the self-sufficient man is seen looking round perplexed upon a world in which all the old evils keep their places in spite of all his legislations and contrivances, turning up always in new forms when he thinks that they have been destroyed; and his voice is heard full of wonder why it is that he has failed. Then comes the failure also of the other idea. Man standing aloof, and expecting to see God redeem the world, sees no such thing. No flash out of the open sky blasts wickedness away; no tempest comes to do the work of purification which man has failed to do. There too there is a lack of faith. Man learns that simply to trust God with expectation that He will do everything while we do nothing is not faith. Then, in the failure of these two ideas about the world's salvation, comes another which is distinctly different from either. Not man alone, and not God alone, is going to purify this world. But man and God, made one by perfect sympathy, by the entire openness of life between them, by perfect love and free gift of himself upon the part of God, by perfect obedience and receptivity upon the part of man, they are the two together—nay, they two together are not two, they are the one which is to make the old world into the new world by the driving out of sin. The principle which makes God and man to be one power is faith. When man has faith in God his nature so opens itself to be filled with God that God and he make a new unity, different at once from pure heavenly divinity and from pure earthly humanity, the new unit of man inspired by God; and by that new unit, that new being, it is that the evil is to be conquered and the world is to be saved.

Can we understand that? Let us take two simple illustrations which may make it plain. Look at the artist's chisel. Most certainly it carves the statue. The artist cannot carve without his chisel. And yet imagine the chisel, conscious that it was made to carve and that that is its function, trying to carve alone. It lays itself against the hard marble, but it has neither strength nor skill; it has no force to drive itself in, and if it had it does not know which way it ought to go. Then we can imagine the chisel full of disappointment. "Why cannot I carve?" it cries. And then the artist comes and seizes it. The chisel lays itself into his hand, and is obedient to him. That obedience is faith. It opens the channels between the sculptor's brain and the hard steel. Thought, feeling, imagination, skill flow down from the deep chambers of the artist's soul to the chisel's edge. The sculptor and the chisel are not two, but one. It is the unit which they make that carves the statue.

Look at the army and its great commander. The army tries to fight the battle, and is routed. Then its scattered regiments gather themselves together, and put themselves into the hands of the great general and obey him perfectly, and fight the battle once more and succeed. "Why could not I succeed?" the army cries, and the general answers, "Because of your unbelief. Because you had no faith. You separated yourself from me. You are but half a power, not a whole power. The power which has won the battle now is not you and is not I; it is made up of you and me together, and the power which made us a unit was your obedient faith."

In both these illustrations we can see, I think,

how it is that the condition comes of which I spoke at first, the condition of man ever surprised at his own failures and haunted by visions of success. Must not that be just the condition of the chisel out of the sculptor's hand, if we let our imagination clothe it with a dim tool-like consciousness? It feels what it was made for; its sharp edge hungers for the marble; it dreams of statues; it is bewildered when it finds it has no power to fulfil its dreams. And so the army dreams of victories, and wonders why it lingers in the camp, or why, if it goes into the fight, it is driven routed from the field. Are they not perfect pictures of the faithless man, of man, that is, out of the hand of God, who yet feels in himself the unaccomplished purpose of his life, who dreams of moral triumphs, and after a thousand moral failures is still surprised for ever that he does not succeed.

This is our principle, then. The unit of power for moral victory—in other words, for goodness—on the earth is not man and is not God. It is God and man, not two but one, not meeting accidentally, not running together in emergencies only to separate again when the emergency is over; it is God and man belonging essentially together, God filling man, man opening his life by faith to be a part of God's, as the gulf opens itself and is part of the great ocean. Is that a fancy and a theory? I pity the man whose life has not made him see two things: first, that if such a union of God and man could come to pass; if man could open his feebleness by faith for God to fill with strength; if God could find in man the perfectly obedient fulfiller of His righteousness, the work would all be done; the problem of evil would be solved; sin, wretchedness, war, lust, would vanish from the earth, and man's imperfectness remain only as the bright road, not yet travelled but full of certain promise of delight, by which man should for ever and for ever come nearer to his God. And second, that man surely has a power of faith, a power of opening his life and being filled by God, which he has thus far used just enough to prove that it exists, but whose wonderful capacity he has yet to discover. When a man's life has given him profoundly these two convictions, then he must look forward and dream of, even if he does not clearly anticipate, a time in which man, with his whole nature wide open to God, shall make with God a unity which shall subdue the world for goodness, when not man's wish to make the world a more convenient place to live in, but the higher and diviner wish to make the world a mirror of the righteousness of God, shall at last cast out the devils which have rent the world so long. And when a man lets his soul even dream of such a consummation there come to him reassuring glimpses of its possibility in the light of many a faithful life which, just in proportion to its faith, is seen to be filled with the power of God and casts the devils out of the little world in which it lives.

I know that it may seem as if in speaking thus I seemed in some way to dishonour God; but it is not so. "Man does need God," some one will say; "but is it also true that God needs man?" And yet, in saying that, we must remember that we are only saying what the Bible says continually. God has so built his world that it is through man as the normal and ordinary means that He does much of His work upon fellow-man. He no doubt still keeps in His own hands the power of direct influence. By means of miracle He may step in and do without man that which man is not faithful enough to allow to be done through Him. But still the Bible rings with the call of God to man, bidding him come "to the help of the Lord, to the help of the Lord against the mighty." We may dismiss that thought, I think. The man who submissively puts himself in God's hand to be an instrument of His designs will certainly become so humbly conscious that the power is in God and not in him, that he will never think that God is dishonoured by using such an instrument as he is for His work. It is he that is glorified, and not God who is degraded or accounted weak.

And if we really want to realise the relation, surely it is not hard. We have its picture in the relation which man holds to Nature. In its degree, so far as it is in its power, the relation of man to Nature illustrates perfectly the relation which man holds to God. Just as man, even the feeblest man, works in conformity with the laws of Nature, he is strong. Just as man, even the strongest man, tries to work in disobedience to the laws of Nature, he is weak. The little child brings flame to wood and the wood kindles; the wisest scholar or the strongest giant brings flame and stone together, and the stone will not burn. The ignorant doctor comes to the sick man and tries to cure him. All his unskilful treatment fails; the fever still continues; the hot blood will not cool; the angry pestilence still rages. Then (is it not the story of Mount Tabor over again?) Nature, sublime and calm, comes down out of the mountain and touches the sick man, and says to the disease, "Begone," and the sick man is well. And then the doctor, if he be as wise and as humble as the Lord's disciples, goes to Nature apart and asks the old question, "Why could not

I cast it out?" And Nature answers just as Jesus answered, "Because of your unbelief. You had not faith in me. You worked by yourself. You were shut up by ignorance or self-content, so that I could not flow into you. You and I together ought to have cured that man. You could not do it without me. It might be that I could do it without you; but the true force that should have done it should have been you and I together, you filled with me, I operative through you; you and I making one force." Lift that discourse out of its crude impersonality; let the dream of Nature be turned into the reality of God, and is not all our doctrine there? The power which is to subdue the world and drive the devils out is made of God and man, united perfectly by love and faith, and made one power, speaking strong words before which no monstrous usurper on the earth should dare to stand a moment.

Oh, how the history of the world has lost this truth! Now with a faithless manhood which felt no need and claimed no presence of Divinity, the fight against misery and sin has been carried on. Now, thinking that God would do it all and that man had no place in the great work, an impractical religion has stood by and waited for a miraculous cleansing of the earth which never came. Some day the perfect power—God using an entirely obedient manhood, man perfectly obedient and only asking to be used by God—these two together, not two but one, God in man and man in God, shall come, and then the world's salvation draweth nigh,—nay, is already here!

As I say this, do I not know whither the hearts of many of you leap at once? Do I not hear you say, "That has come. That has been on the earth already, and is here now in Him who, once living, is alive for evermore. God in man and man in God! Why, that is the Incarnation! that is Jesus Christ!" Indeed it is, my friends. Oh, how it lifts us away above the often petty discussions of the marvellous nature of Christ when we come clearly to the sight of this, that in Him certainly there was the fulfilment of that which, when men try to conceive of what the world needs most, is the complete expression of their fullest dreams—man in God and God in man : the Divine and human perfectly reconciled, perfectly united—not two forces, but one force! That was the Christ who went from haunt to haunt of the devils and bade them flee ; and they, the devils of hatred, cruelty, lust, selfishness, brutishness, superstition,—they all fled at His presence. And now to fill the earth with Himself, that is His wish and purpose, that is what He is labouring for through all these slow discouraging centuries in which, beneath the turmoil and distress upon the surface, the watchful ear can never fail to hear below the sounds which tell us that He is still at work. What is the real meaning of His purpose? Is He not trying to make His brethren what He was, to assert in them as it was asserted in Him, that it is an Incarnation, a God in man that is to save the world? We talk about Christ's second coming. Whatever else it may include, must it not certainly include that—the Incarnation realised throughout all the world—man everywhere with his life opened by faith and filled with God, able to take to himself the words of the Incarnate Christ: "I and my Father are one;" "My Father worketh and I work;" "Whatsoever things the Father doeth, these also doeth the Son likewise"? The Incarnation of God in Jesus repeated and fulfilled in the occupation of a faithful and obedient humanity by God, that is the promised salvation of the world.

I want to turn, in what time now remains, to a more personal application of all that I have been saying to the immediate lives of those who hear me. There are many men here, many young men, who know something of what it is to struggle with their sins. It is strange how the aspect of that struggle changes as a man goes on in life. Here is a man who year by year has been growing aware that some sin was getting possession of him.

Whatever it might be—intemperance, untruthfulness, impurity, selfishness, idleness—whenever he has looked up across his character in self-survey, he has seen the tents in which that vice was encamped grown a little more abundant and more bold, just as a farmer on his great western farm might see the huts of the intruders growing thicker on his land. The vice has grown bolder and more familiar. It has not hid itself away in the valleys; it has climbed more and more to the hill-tops of the life, and taken possession of its richest fields. All the time the man has been saying to himself, "Some morning I will rouse myself and drive this intruder out. I know this vice is wicked and disgraceful; it shall not be always there. Some day I will gather up my manly strength and sweep the whole base thing away." Well, at last the day came. Something or other, some more than usually flagrant insolence of the intrusive vice, some yet more audacious attempt to occupy some choicer and more sacred fields, some momentary glimpse of what the end must be, some revelation from the best judgment of his fellow-men—something or other opened the man's eyes and made him say to himself that now that vice must go. Do you not know the easy confidence with which he made his resolution? Can you not see him starting out upon his expedition as if he went forth to a summer's frolic? And then, oh, my friends, do not many of you know perfectly, by your own experience, what came next? Can you not remember the surprise, the disappointment, the dismay with which you found that the vice had become a part of your very life, and would not be ordered away? The tree which you thought you could pluck up and cast over the fence in an instant had its roots around your very heart. It is wonderful what that discovery brings to a man. If he is not much in earnest, if he is only playing at self-reform, it brings an end of all his effort. "Well, let it stay," he says; "if it really is a part of me, I cannot help it. Perhaps it is not so bad as I thought it was." But if he is in earnest, then the very persistency of the vice makes it seem all the more dreadful. The discovery of how hard it is to give up drink makes the brutality of drink look all the more horrible. Never did purity appear so precious as when the libertine finds how the poison of impurity has entered into his very soul. Along with his horror there is a strange surprise. The unnaturalness of sin is felt all the more as the intense hold of sin on him grows clear. It seems every moment as if he must be free and yet every moment the struggle grows more hopeless. Surprise and fear blend in the soul's cry as it perseveres in its almost desperate wrestling with the sin which has fastened itself upon its life—"Why cannot I, oh, why cannot I, cast him out?"

And then what comes? Oh, it is noble and pathetic, it is an everlasting testimony of the essential childship of the human heart, that always then man turns to God. Overcome with surprise and terror at its own defeat, the heart takes its task and carries it and lays it upon God. "Thou, O God, must save me, for I cannot save myself." It is a noble impulse. Its perpetual recurrence is the most significant thing in all the life of man. It is not strange if sometimes—very often—it should be distorted; it is not strange that very often the poor man, baffled and defeated in his own attempt to cast his sins away, turns to God, as if in Him there were some power on which the whole work could be laid, and which, without the man's co-operation, might do for him what he had so failed to do for himself. But there is no power such as that in God; not even God can cast a man's sins away except with the cordial co-working of the sinful man himself. I dare not preach to any sinner here that there is nothing for him to do—nothing but to stand still and watch, as if it were another man's experience that he were watching, while God takes his sin out of him and makes him pure. Sin is too true a part of the soul which has once let sin into it for that. And what then?

Not by our own struggle, and not by a purely external help of God. What then? Only by the new unit of power which is made of you and God in reconciliation and co-operation. Do you not see? Just as the world is to be saved at last by a humanity perfectly united with God through obedience, of which the Incarnation of Jesus Christ was both the type and the means, so you are to be saved by the confederacy of your nature with God's nature in the true submission of your will to His. You want to escape from the slavery of drink. You cannot do it by mere resolution, as if you and the power of drink were the only two beings who came at all into the question; you cannot do it by simply calling on God to come and release you, and standing by yourself to see Him do the miracle; but by lifting up yourself until you can put your will into the hands of His will as an instrument, by putting yourself into His revelation of what you really are, by saying, "Lord, save me; here am I to save myself with; oh, use me for my own salvation!" So, my dear friends, so, and so alone, you can be saved.

One man comes and says, "I have been very wicked; now I am going to turn over a new leaf and make myself very good." Another man comes and says, "I am very wicked, but I have prayed to God, and He will make me good." Oh, how often we have heard them both; how often both of them have failed. Then comes another man. Already, before he speaks, you can see in his face a mingled determination and humility in which you recognise the real strength. He says, "I have given myself to Christ, that with me He may save me. I have put my will into the power of His love and holiness, that, wielded by them, it may be fit to fight with and to kill these sins of mine." There is the man, you know, who will succeed. Before him the glorious new life of freedom from sin already opens with sure promise.

True, in our story Christ, when He came and found the disciples helpless before their task, did put forth His hand and healed the sick boy with no help of theirs. But that was an exceptional event, what we call a miracle. The great method of His operation when it was thoroughly established was to work through obedient men. And here, it was not for the disciples themselves but for the poor lunatic that the healing was required. When he had work to do in them their own wills always must co-operate. It was Matthew's obedience in the hand of Christ's commandment that saved Matthew. It was Paul's consecration in the hand of Christ's grace that did the work of Paul.

So it must be in any world which our imagination can conceive or which Revelation has revealed. No world can there be anywhere where God can purify or save a soul by mere omnipotence; none where the soul must not itself give itself up in labour for its own salvation before it can be saved; none also, we dare to believe, where, as long as sin shall last, all that shall not be possible; none where souls may not turn and, giving themselves to God, give Him the chance to save them.

But not for any future world let that conversion be delayed. Now is the time! Now is the day! Oh, my dear people, if any of you are struggling with your sins, I beg you to learn the truth and see it wholly. You cannot cast them out, but if you will give yourself to Him He can cast them out with you. Hate your sins for His sake; hate them not merely because they make you poor and wretched, but because they do Him dishonour; crave holiness because it is both His will and your own truest nature; let His love fill you with love, and then the conquering of your sins by His help shall be in its course one long enthusiasm and at the end a glorious success. That is your hope, and that hope, if you will, you may seize to-day.

X.

NATURE AND CIRCUMSTANCES.[1]

"Verily I say unto you, Among them that are born of women there hath not risen a greater than John the Baptist: notwithstanding he that is least in the kingdom of heaven is greater than he."—MATTHEW xi. 11.

IT is Jesus who is talking about John the Baptist; and the question of which He is speaking is one that must have almost necessarily arisen with regard to two such teachers. Jesus had come to establish on the earth a higher life for man. He had been telling men that they must enter into the new spiritual culture, which, while it was the sequel and fulfilment of the education of the world which had gone before, was yet indeed new in Him, was the creation of His personal nature and His revelation of God. He was engaged in setting up the kingdom of God, into which all the servants of God were to be gathered, and where their lives were to be trained. And in the midst of this

[1] Preached in Lincoln Cathedral, Sunday morning, 24th June 1883.

great work it could not be but that men would look around and would look back. Jesus was telling them that the true greatness of human life must come by following Him. It was inevitable, then, that men should ask, "How is it about those great men who are not His followers; those great men who have gone before Him; those great men who are wholly outside of His influence—are they not truly great? And if they are, what has become of His saying that true greatness lies only in Him, and in the kingdom of God to which He is so earnestly summoning us?" This was the question that must have come into many minds as Jesus spoke. To this question Jesus gave His answer—"Among them that are born of women there hath not risen a greater than John the Baptist: notwithstanding he that is least in the kingdom of heaven is greater than he." Because the question which brought forth this answer is not obsolete, but is on men's minds in many shapes to-day, I propose to you that we should study Christ's answer for a while this morning.

And notice, first, that it is a question which belongs not to the things of Christ, nor to religious things alone. All life suggests it; for in all life there are these two ways of estimating the probable value of men—one by the direct perception of their characters, the other by the examination of the institutions to which they belong, and the privileges which they enjoy. Think of the schoolboy who is just graduating from one of our public schools, and of Socrates who died more than two thousand years ago in Greece. The schoolboy represents the privileged condition which is the result of centuries of civilisation. Knowledge has been offered him every day, on every page of his school-books, of which the great Greek sage never dreamed; facts are trite commonplaces to him, before whose slightest suggestion Socrates would have stood and laughed at their impossibility. The privilege of the schoolboy's life is manifest enough. The dullest boy in all the class cannot help knowing things which were utterly out of the power of the ancient philosopher. And what then? Is the schoolboy greater than Socrates? In one sense certainly he is: greater in the richness of circumstance, in the opportunity of knowledge, in the profusion and luxuriance of life; but the moment that we ask the question, there stands out at once the personal greatness of the great man, which no distance of time can dim, and no inferiority of circumstances can disguise. The schoolboy dwindles to a grain of sand beside the mountain of his lofty genius. These are the two evident facts. The schoolboy belongs to a higher order, a higher range of life, and so is greater in his circumstances, in the necessity of his condition; but the philosopher is greater in himself, unspeakably, immeasurably greater in his personal genius. How shall we describe it better than in some echo of the words which Jesus spoke about John the Baptist. The philosopher is among the very greatest of historic men; but the least of modern men has that which he, with all his greatness, could not have.

Here, then, we see the two elements: there is the greatness of nature, and there is the greatness of circumstances. They are distinct from one another; they do not make each other. A man may be great in nature and yet live among the meagrest surroundings. A man may live in the most sumptuous profusion of privileges, and yet be a very little man. They are distinct. One does not make the other; and yet the two have close relations; each has a tendency towards the production of the other. The higher plane of living is always trying to make the man greater, so that he may be worthy of it; and, on the other hand, the more the man grows great, the more he struggles to discover and attain some higher plane of life. In every fullest picture of human life the two combine; the great man in the fullest atmosphere alone entirely satisfies our imagination. But if they must be separated, as to some degree they always must, nothing can destroy the honour which belongs to personal character struggling under the most adverse circumstances to assert its greatness and to do its work.

But now, if these definitions have made the conditions of the problem plain, we are ready to go on to the truth which is included in what Christ says about John the Baptist. Christ recognises the two elements of personal greatness and of lofty condition, and He seems almost to suggest another truth, which is at any rate familiar to our experience of life, which is that personal power which has been manifest in some lower region of life seems sometimes to be temporarily lost and dimmed with the advance of the person who possesses it into a higher condition. What really is a progress seems, for a time at least, to involve a loss. Think how this appears in our observation of the world. The college student graduates next week, and from the calm seclusion of scholastic life he goes out into the wrestling with business forces or the eager rivalry of his profession. He has really passed up into a higher life; but sometimes he looks back and sighs for the peace and dignity which the old life enjoyed. The thinker, anywhere, tries to apply his thought, and though the contact with men, into which that effort brings him, disturbs his equanimity and throws him into perplexities which he knew nothing of before, he too has really mounted to a higher life. The æsthetic student tries to be useful ; and it is only through painful shocks to his sensibilities, and a disturbance of the symmetry of life in which his soul delights, that he passes into the loftier condition where he can help his fellow-men. Everywhere that which seems to have perfected itself in the lower sphere displays its imperfection when it passes up to higher tasks. Thought, which has grown clear and self-complacent in the study of the physical world, bewilders itself and is baffled when it attempts to study God. Government, which seems to have mastered the problems of despotism, loses its equilibrium and is feeble once more when it attempts the higher tasks of freedom.

You remember, perhaps, the noble and beautiful verses in which Robert Browning, standing among the great pictures in Florence, speaks in their behalf across the centuries of the Greek statues which have confessedly a perfectness, an absolute completeness, in their own domain of beauty which the great Christian pictures cannot boast. It is the finiteness of view and purpose of the great classic works which gives them the chance to be complete :—

"To-day's brief passion limits their range,
 It seethes with the morrow for us and more.

> They are perfect—how else? they shall never change:
> We are faulty—why not? we have time in store.
> The Artificer's hand is not arrested
> With us—we are rough-hewn, no-wise polished:
> They stand for our copy, and, once invested
> With all they can teach, we shall see them abolished."

It is a strange perplexing fact of life, this fact that as a being or a work, which has seemed perfect in some lower region, goes up to some higher region, it seems to grow imperfect; at least it manifests its imperfection. We can see at once what a temptation it must offer to the human powers to linger in some lower sphere, in which they seem to be equal to their work, instead of going freely up into a loftier world where they shall learn their limitations and their feebleness. There is reason enough to fear that man's power of thought, revelling to-day in the clearness with which it seems to see the lower world of physical existence, will refuse some of the higher duties which belong to it, the duties which most tax its capacity and show its feebleness, the duties of understanding the soul of man and reaching after the comprehension of God. Sad will it be if it is so; if studious humanity, delighted with its achievements in the mere region of physical research, shall turn its back on the lofty tasks in which man's intellect finds its greatest glory as well as its most complete humility—the struggle to know God.

In ordinary life the power of this temptation, the temptation to be satisfied with greatness in some lower sphere and not to aspire to the highest sort of existence, is constantly appearing. What multitudes of men there are all through society who seem to have limited and shut in their lives to some little range of occupations which they can fulfil with reasonable credit to themselves, and never seem to think that there is any call for them to do more than to complete themselves in that poor little scheme of life, never seem to dream that they ought to go up to a distinctly other life with higher tasks and more difficult exactions. An idle, good-natured creature, who has accepted his place and fills it, who amuses and is amused, who keeps the world about him in good-humour, and is great in the adornment of his own person and the management of petty etiquette; one of the coolest things on earth, I think, is the quiet effrontery with which such a man rests absolutely satisfied with his insect greatness, and criticises the blunders and feebleness which men of course develop who are setting themselves to do some really useful work in the world. He treats them and talks of them as if they belonged to a different world from his, and there could be no possible call for him to undertake the same effort with all its risks and exposures. One of the most wonderful things in the world is this power of men to draw themselves a line beyond which they never dream of counting themselves responsible, across which they look and judge with cruellest criticisms the men who are really fighting the world's sins and troubles on the other side, as if of them there were no more to be asked than just that they should be perfect in their own self-limited world of elegant uselessness. Never a brave reformer tries to break down a popular sin or to build up some new and needed progress, taking on himself the responsibility which a true man ought to take, but these self-satisfied critics gather around him to criticise his methods and to ridicule his blunders, but never lift a hand to show how they too would blunder if they let themselves step outside of their safe and limited and petty life.

This, I think, is the way in which most men of the world look at Christianity and at the efforts of their brother men to live a Christian life. " I am no Christian," says the practical man ; " I do not pretend to be pious or religious." And then he looks up in your face as if he had settled the whole question, as if his entire business thenceforth were just to stand by and see what sort of a

Christian you were and how your piety came on. "I do my duty as a plain unreligious man," he says ; "I make no professions." There is a tone of scornful pity as he speaks. He realises—but not more keenly than the poor Christian realises himself—how the believer in Christ, the man who is trying to honour and obey a Divine Master, stumbles and blunders in his attempt to keep company with the Infinite. For himself he has abandoned any such attempt, and seems by some strange self-delusion to have brought himself to feel that his abandonment of the attempt has released him from any responsibility about it. You see how foolish and how base such a position is. It is the soldier who has shirked the battle criticising the torn uniform and broken armour and bleeding limbs of his comrade who comes staggering out of the fight. It is the ship which has lain snugly and uselessly beside the wharf jeering at the broken bulwarks and torn sails with which its sister ship comes reeling in from her long voyage. He who lingers in some lower life because there he is able to keep his complacency and not to fall so far short of his manifest duty as to cover himself with shame, has no right to compare himself with the feeblest and most unsuccessful of the children of God, who, unable to be satisfied as long as there is a spiritual life which he is not living, has set boldly forth and entered at least into the outskirts of the kingdom of heaven, into the determination and struggle to live a religious life.

There must be some such people here to-day. There must be some men here who are satisfied with doing their duty in some lower sphere of life and leaving the higher spheres entirely untouched, satisfied to be honest in business and kind to their families and pure in their daily lives, and leaving unattempted the whole effort to know God and to live in communion with Him, as if they had no more call to deal with that region of life than they have to go up and walk among the stars. Surely they must see that that is not a perfect life. Surely, when they have once caught sight of it, that higher unappropriated region of living, that unentered kingdom of heaven must entice them with an invitation which will not let them rest. No true man can live a half life when he has genuinely learned that it is only a half life. The other half, the higher half, must haunt him. God grant that it may haunt every one of you until he arises and insists on the fulfilment of his life by the cordial and enthusiastic acceptance of the obedience of God.

One puzzles himself sometimes in the attempt to grasp the entire meaning of those great words of Christ to Nicodemus. "You must be born again," the Master said. Does not the substance of its meaning lie in the truth of which I have been speaking? Nicodemus wanted Christ to meet him in a lower world, a world of moral precepts and Hebrew traditions, where the Pharisee was thoroughly at home. But Christ said, "No, there is a higher world; you must go up there; you must enter into that; you must have a new birth and live in a new life,—in a life where God is loved and known and trusted and communed with. Not merely a better life of the old kind, but a new kind of life. Except you be born again, you cannot see the kingdom of God, which is that new kind of life; and he who is least in that kingdom, he who has in any degree begun to live that higher kind of life has something which the best and noblest soul in the inferior life has not, is greater than the greatest who is not in the kingdom."

The progress from one kind of life into a higher kind, from one realm into a yet deeper and more central region of God's kingdom, is always pressing; it can never be outgrown. Not merely when a man becomes a Christian, but always afterwards when some deeper and holier and maturer region of Christian life opens before him, the summons comes to move on, to advance into that higher realm. When the religion which has been living on mere authority is called upon to become a religion of clear personal conviction; when to the religion of sentiment is offered the test and privilege of active duty; when the religion of the single experience is bidden to graduate into a wide human sympathy,—in all these cases, the same sort of thing occurs which occurs when the man of the world is first summoned to enter into the kingdom of heaven, to become a Christian. The door of a new room of life is thrown open, and the soul which has lived faithfully in the first room is bidden not to rest satisfied with that faithfulness, but to pass on into the second. May God give us grace and faith and courage and ambition always to be ready for that call, and to pass on and up to higher kinds of life, to new kingdoms of heaven as He shall open them to us for ever.

And now, in the remainder of this sermon I want to dwell upon another application of our truth which I cannot help hoping may throw some light upon a question which I know has puzzled many of us. I want to see how it applies to the explanation and understanding of a true and noble life lived in a false faith. Many of you recognise that question, I am sure. You have encountered its bewilderment. Perhaps you are encountering it now. Here is a creed which you know to be false, or to be wofully imperfect : it either denies or it ignores the truths which you know are supremely true. And here is a man who holds this false or this imperfect faith : he either asserts what you are sure is bitter error, or else he denies what you are sure is precious truth. And that man is a good man. He is a great deal better man than you are. His life makes you ashamed. He is generous, brave, pure, unselfish. His character shines like a star. Every one who sees it is better and stronger for the sight. Do you not know the bewilderment which comes ? Do you not know the questions which such a sight suggests ? Is, then, my faith mistaken, or is all faith a matter of no consequence ? Are faith and character totally indifferent to each other ? Has faith no influence on life ? These are the first questions. They are full of darkness. The lighting-up comes when we see that there are really two elements, the man's own personality and his conditions. To make the highest man both of these must be complete. In the case we have supposed, the personality is noble, but, if you are right, the conditions are very faulty. The real question concerning that friend of yours is not, How does he in his unbelief compare with you in your belief? but, How does he in his unbelief compare with what he, the same man, would be if he believed? Ask yourself that question about your noble atheist, or your pure-minded, lofty-hearted heretic, and I think you will surely give yourself the answer that, however beautiful that soul may seem to you now, you know that, touched by the faith of Christ, there is a distinct new beauty, another kind of grace and exaltation which it certainly would win.

It seems to me to be very much like the question of the place of a man's residence. You, an Englishman, full of the sense of privilege which belongs to your country's place in the front rank of civilisation, send your pity across the seas to Africa or Asia. To live there seems to you a dreadful thing. The ignorance of barbarism or the corruption of decaying civilisation are dreadful even to the thought. But as you congratulate yourself upon your privilege, you happen to hear the story of some savage life. You are told of one of those rare natures which shine every now and then in the heart of barbarism: a man brave, generous, tender, conscientious, true. What is the result? Do you throw away all your claims? Do you say England is no better than Africa? What ought to be the result? Is it not very clear? A new and deeper honour for this humanity of ours which will not wait for favourable circumstances, but even from the most unfavourable soils will throw up here and there its choicest flowers ; a deep shame at the thought of how our civilisation has failed of very much which it ought to have done ; but at the same time a clear sense that the best influences of civilisation might have made of that noble savage a far nobler being even than we see him now, and a renewed conviction, enforced even by the sight of this notable exception, that civilisation on the whole makes finer men than barbarism. The sight of the savage's nobleness enlarges my thought of humanity, awakens my shame for the defects of civilisation, but does not make me want to turn African myself, nor to call upon the world to go back into the jungle.

Now why should it not be just exactly so when I see the noble life of a man whose faith I believe is all wrong, or is wofully imperfect. Let me not dare to say that his is not true nobleness. That confuses my moral standards and throws me into the worst hopelessness. Let the sight of him give me a new faith in the power of human nature to be generous and good, which can break through the most oppressive circumstances, and open into flower out of the most barren soils. Let it make me ashamed of the small show of generosity and goodness which I with my better faith am able to display ; but let it not delude me into saying that what I know is my better and fuller faith is a thing of no consequence; let it not hide from me the fact that my infidel friend with all his excellence would be a finer and nobler man than his own present self if he believed in the truth and lived in the power of that which I know to be the faith of God; let it not lead me to forget that the real power of a faith is to be estimated not by the influence of its presence or its absence in individuals who may be exceptional, but by its effect upon broad stretches of human history over wide areas of time and space.

My dear friends, I do believe that this is the simple truth which a good many puzzled people among us need to know. The Christian, with his unbelieving friend, whose daily life, so pure, upright, and honest, shames the poor, half-discouraged believer every day,—what can you say to him? First bid him rejoice that his Christ can and does do for that friend of his so much even while that friend denies Him. Then bid him see that if that friend of his could consciously know and cordially acknowledge the Christ who is doing so much for him already, he would give that Christ a chance to do still more which now He cannot do. Then let him for himself be filled with an inspiring shame which shall make him determined to be worthier of his higher faith. This is the true ministry which ought to come to any Christian from the presence of a man who believes far less than he does, and is a far better man than he is.

You can see at once how all of this must tell upon the whole idea of Christian missions. There may have been a time—though I think more and more that nothing is so delusive as the attempt to realise and restate the religious notions of our fathers—there may perhaps have been a day when, in order to make it seem right for the Christian world to send missionaries to the heathen, it required to be made out that all heathen virtue was a falsehood and delusion. That day is past, if ever it existed. But one of the first results of a cordial acceptance of the idea that human nature even in the depths of pagan darkness does feel the power of God and send forth noble lives, has been to stir the question whether, if that were so, we need, or even whether we ought, to send them Christianity. There have, beyond all doubt, been glorious self-sacrifices, saintly embodiments of purity, shining instances of spiritual aspirations in classic heathenism, and even in barbarian idol-worship. Shall we to systems out of which such lives can come offer our Christianity as their necessary hope, their one complete salvation? Is there not light upon this question in our thoughts of this morning? May not the Christian world stand glorying in every outbreak of the heathen's goodness as a sign of the power with which his Christ, even unknown, may fill a human life which in the very darkness of its ignorance is obedient to whatever best spiritual force it feels? May not that very sight reveal to him what that aspiring heathenism might become if it could be made aware of the Christ whom it is in its unconsciousness obeying—as the very sight of the dim beauty in which the earth lies before the sunrise fills us with hopes and visions of what it will be when the glory of the noon is all ablaze upon it? May not the Christian, even while he goes out to tell the heathen his completer gospel, be filled with an inspiring shame at his own poor use and exhibition of the power of that gospel which he offers to the heathen world? This is the true attitude of Christendom to paganism. It is not arrogant; it brings no insult; it comes like brother to brother, full of honour for the nature to which it offers the larger knowledge of the Father's life. To such broad missionary impulse as that let us be sure that the increase of rational and spiritual Christianity will only add ever new and stronger impulse and inspiration.

The truth which underlies all that I have said this morning seems to me to be very clear and most important. It is the truth that behind every system or dispensation for the education of human life and character lies human life and character itself; and that, however the dispensation may be needed to bring man to his best, his powers and so his responsibilities are there before the dispensation comes to do its work. This is true even of the supreme dispensation of the manifestation of God in Jesus Christ. By that alone can man fulfil his life, and yet before that comes, man in the twilight has the capacity for noble living, and so is bound to attain it. And yet his attainment of noble living anterior to Christianity does not relieve him of the duty or deprive him of the privilege of taking the full revelation of God which is offered to him when at last Christ comes. This is, I think, the teaching of the Saviour when He says, "Of them that are born of women there hath not risen a greater than John the Baptist : notwithstanding he that is least in the kingdom of heaven is greater than he."

It would be easy to see how this truth applies to the relation which man holds to all the highest institutions and dispensations for his spiritual life. It applies to the Church, to the Lord's Supper, to the attainment of assured and certain faith about religious things. I must not dwell upon these special applications, but only in one last word beg you to see how true and strong, how satisfied and yet how expectant a life in general this truth involves. No blindness or deprivation of opportunity in which you live, oh, my friend, deprives you of the right and duty of being a good man. Remember that, and never dare forget it. And yet no power to be a good man in the darkness gives you a right to shut your eyes to any light which God may offer you to lead you to the heights of some new land of goodness where you may be a better man. That is the faith which makes a man work earnestly and joyously upon the earth, yet never losing out of his sight the promised heaven, and so being ready for every summons to come up higher which the Master sends—always ready for the final welcome: "Thou hast been faithful over a few things, I will make thee ruler over many things: enter thou into the joy of thy Lord."

XI.

THE WILLING SURRENDER.[1]

"Thinkest thou that I cannot now pray to my Father, and he shall presently give me more than twelve legions of angels? But how then shall the scriptures be fulfilled, that thus it must be?"—MATTHEW xxvi. 53.

IN his epistle to the Philippians St. Paul gives a very earnest exhortation to his disciples, setting the example of their Master before them in a wonderful way. "Let this mind be in you," he says, "which was also in Christ Jesus: who, being in the form of God, thought it not robbery to be equal with God: but made Himself of no reputation, and took upon Him the form of a servant, and was made in the likeness of men." The glory of Christ is in His willing surrender of that which belonged to Him, and which He might have always had and enjoyed. It is certainly interesting to find Christ Himself dwelling on this same fact in His history of which His disciple speaks. It is

[1] Preached at the church of St. Peter-at-Arches, Lincoln, Sunday evening, 24th June 1883.

in the Garden of Gethsemane. The multitude whom the chief priests had sent was just arresting Jesus. Then one of His disciples drew his sword and showed resistance. But Jesus bade him put his sword into its place again. He tells His eager follower that if He wants to He can protect Himself: "Thinkest thou that I cannot now pray to my Father, and He shall presently give me more than twelve legions of angels?" But then He thinks of how the work He has to do makes such escape impossible. He waves the thought aside : " But how then should the scriptures be fulfilled, that thus it must be?" For a moment it seems as if the helpless prisoner, held tight there between His enemies, looked up and saw the air thick with angels hurrying down to His relief. The grip upon His arms grew loose ; He heard his Father's voice behind the angels commanding them to save Him. Their bright swords flashed around Him, and he was free and safe. All this was not an impossible dream ; it was something that might be true. A word of His might summon it. For an instant the word seems almost to be trembling on His lips. But then He says to Himself, "No, I must not. I came to do things which I could not do if I should let myself do this. I have the power, but I will not use it ; " and so He shuts His eyes upon the vision of the angels, and goes on to the trial and the scourging and the cross.

"Let this mind be in us," said Christ's apostle, "which was also in Christ Jesus." I want you to think this evening of the nobleness of this surrender of Jesus, and of the way in which no man becomes really noble who has not somehow its repetition in himself. The act itself which I have pictured must stir any generous soul. Christ, with freedom and honour waiting at His call, quietly shutting His lips and refusing to call them, and going on into suffering and shame,—that is one of the scenes which we may make a test-scene of human character. The man who calls that voluntary self-surrender foolish shows that he is himself ignoble. Everything that there is noble in a man's nature leaps up to honour it; and everywhere, where the mind which was in Christ Jesus has been in any other man, that other man's brethren have felt his nobleness. To give up some precious thing which is legitimately yours; to shut your eyes upon visions of glory or safety or luxury which you might make your own without a shade of blame, that is so truly one of the marks of nobleness that no man is accounted by the best standards truly noble who is not doing that in some degree. The man who is taking all that he has a right to take in life is always touched with a suspicion and a shade of baseness. There is a paradox in it, no doubt; one of those moral paradoxes which make the world of moral study always fascinating. Man has no right to take his full rights in the world; he is not wholly noble unless he sees the higher law which declares that all is not his to take which is his legitimately to own. Let us try to study this nobleness of voluntary surrender a little while to-night.

And first, we want to feel how definite and distinct it is. There are base imitations of it with which we must not let it be confounded. There are two different kinds of renunciation of things which we have the right and power to possess which have their origin in motives which are unworthy of our human nature and degrade it. Let us look at each of them for a moment or two before we turn to the noble and ennobling renunciation from which they must always be distinguished.

The first of the two is the renunciation which comes from idleness or lack of spirit. There will always be people, there are people among us, who might be rich or learned or famous, who despise wealth or fame or learning simply because of the trouble which they involve; and such a man often seems to himself, and seems sometimes to his friends, to be doing something fine and heroic in standing outside of the rush and hurly-burly of human life, and with the superior air of a spectator who is on the other side of the ropes watching and criticising the wrestlers who are struggling in the race. In the curious world of college life, one of the constant characters is the man who might do anything, and does absolutely nothing. He is in every class; he always has been, and he always will be—the man who is supposed to be voluntarily withholding the hand which, if he chose to stretch it out, might easily pluck the highest honours. He is probably always more or less of a fraud. If he exerted himself he would be found to be very much like other men; and the reason why he does not exert himself is not that he is above, but that he is below the ambitions which incite his fellows. In the world of faith there are always men who abandon thinking, that they may escape the disturbance of their opinions. They praise themselves, other men perhaps praise them, because they have no doubts, but surely the surrender which they make is a loss and not a gain, a disgrace and not an honour. Everywhere we must discriminate. Such renunciations as these have nothing in common with the divine relinquishment of Jesus. Vastly, vastly better is the most eager, headlong, passionate pursuit of reputation, comfort, learning, truth, than this abandonment of struggle, which means nothing but laziness and torpor.

The second of the two base forms of voluntary surrender is what we may call in general the ascetic form. It includes all those renunciations of legitimate employments and enjoyments which are made directly and purely for the effect of such renunciations on ourselves—either that we may be mortified and chastened by disappointment, or that an appetite for some desirable thing may be whetted by restraint. It is under this last motive that many people seem to feel as if even religion and the service of God would suffer if it were made too common, if it were brought close and kept close to human life, if it were made the power by which every least action were to be moved. This sort of renunciation, which really has its source in a certain doubt of the sufficiency of the best things to become a continual experience, is exquisitely expressed in one of the most beautiful of Shakespeare's sonnets, where the withholding of the grasp from what is genuinely in its power is vividly portrayed :—

> " So am I as the rich, whose blessed key
> Can bring him to his sweet up-locked treasure,
> The which he will not every hour survey,
> For blunting the fine point of seldom pleasure.
> Therefore are feasts so solemn and so rare,
> Since, seldom coming, in the long year set,

> Like stones of worth they thinly placed are,
> Or captain jewels in the carcanet.
> So is the time that keeps you as my chest,
> Or as the wardrobe which the robe doth hide,
> To make some special instant special blest,
> By new unfolding his imprison'd pride."

It is far from being a subject upon which good and thoughtful men are agreed. Probably it is a subject on which there will never be complete agreement. Probably the difference of men's natures and temperaments will always make them judge differently regarding it. But to me it seems as if the simply ascetic renunciation of any good and healthy thing,—that is to say, the renunciation of it purely and directly for the effect which its surrender may have upon the character of the man who renounces it, or for the heightening of the value of the thing itself—had an essential unreality about the act, and implied a distrust of the relinquished object which must defeat its own purpose and make the self-surrender worthless.

These, then, are the two kinds of relinquishment which we lay aside and put out of the question. Now turn back again to Jesus. When He said, "I will not call the angels," it was no pusillanimous submitting to His fate; nor was it any unnatural submitting of Himself to suffering that He might be cultivated and purified, or that the release from suffering when it came might be more sweet. There is no such refinement and self-consciousness as that in all His life. It is simply that He has a work to do, and that if the angels come and snatch Him out of the hands of the ruffianly Jews, His work will not get done. Therefore He shuts His eyes upon the angels and closes His lips and will not call them, and is dragged away, to Annas first, and then to Pilate, and then to the cross. It was the quiet surrender of what was truly His, because He could not have it and yet do His work and save the world.

Let us take at once two or three of the most familiar illustrations which we can think of in our ordinary life, and see how there this sort of surrender wins from us all the same sort of honour when we see it in our fellow-men which it has when we see it in our Master Christ. There is one spectacle which never fails to impress a community like that of one of our modern cities, which is largely mercantile in its standards,—a spectacle whose constant recurrence is one of the perpetual illuminations and redemptions of the sordid tendencies of life,—a spectacle, indeed, which it is hard to see how we could spare from among the influences by which the life of a community is kept pure and high. When a man who might be rich deliberately gives up the chance of wealth that he may be a scholar, men whose object in life is wealth, and who know that he has the same power to get wealth which they have if he should give himself to its pursuit, must honour him and feel the influence of his renunciation. It is not laziness, for he goes to work harder than any of them. It is not asceticism, for he has no foolish sweeping abuse of wealth with which to insult his fellow-men's intelligence. It is not incapacity, for he is as bright as the brightest. It is simply the power of a higher purpose. It is the calm, manly, uncomplaining choice to do this greater thing, and to surrender whatever would hinder the doing of it most faithfully and well. The man goes off into his study, and thinks that nobody sees him,—indeed, does not think for a moment whether anybody is seeing him or not; but his life and such lives as his are the salt of the society in which they live.

There is another picture which, when one has his eyes open to discover it, gives a pathetic beauty to many a quiet household with its family life. The land is full of households where the father and mother have no ripe cultivation, have never been able to take time or thought for study and its blessings and delights, but out of which the children come forth furnished with all that the most careful cultivation can bestow, radiant with the happiness and helpfulness of culture. What does it mean? It is not that the father and mother had not the capacity or that they had not the love for learning. They appreciated it; perhaps they lived all their life long in hunger for it. The very careful care with which they provided it for their dearer selves, their children, sending their boys to college while they stayed and worked upon the farm or in the shop at home, shows how they knew the worth of what they did not take themselves. Many a time they looked up and saw the angels only waiting for a word to lift their wings and come; many a time their lips opened impatiently to speak the word; and yet every time they left the word unspoken and turned back to their meagre work again, saying in their hearts, " How then should the scriptures be fulfilled, that thus it must be?" "Is it not written in the scripture of my fatherhood that I must make my child a way into the richest knowledge, even though my own life be laid level with the ground that he may walk over it?" Is there a more beautiful sight in all the earth than that? What triumphant life standing upon the summit of human knowledge and looking wide over all the vast expanse has half the real glory which belongs to the father-life working hard in the darkness at the mountain's foot, and by his hard work making possible that climbing of his son into the celestial light.

In Thomas Carlyle's delightful Reminiscences of his father, which have been published since the great writer's death, there are these beautiful words about the rude and sturdy stonemason from whom he sprang: "I feel to my father—so great though so neglected, so generous also towards me—a strange tenderness, and mingled pity and reverence peculiar to the case, infinitely soft and near my heart. Was he not a sacrifice to me? Had I stood in his place, could he not have stood in mine, and more? Thou good father! well may I for ever honour thy memory. Surely that act was not without its reward. And was not nature great, out of such materials to make such a man?" It is a beautiful and noble tribute, but as we read it we are ready, I think, to feel that the man who could deserve it was even greater than the man who could write it.

No man in this world has a right to all his rights; that is the paradox which states our truth. It often seems as if the highest and profoundest truths could not be stated except in paradox. "If one is always claiming his rights," says a German author, "the world is like a hell." Here is really the key to that question about voluntary abstinence from certain innocent indulgences for the sake of other people, which is a very pressing question to many people in our time, a question whose prominence indeed in our time is one of the most interesting symptoms of the moral condition which the world has reached. We may be sure that it is no low condition of moral life in which men are constantly urging upon themselves and upon one another abstinence from pleasures which in themselves are perfectly legitimate, because of the influence which free indulgence in those pleasures might have upon other people. And it is hard to think that any person of awakened moral sense in days like these does not recognise this duty of the sacrifice of things to which, looking only at themselves and at him, he has a most indisputable right. It is in the matter of temperance, so called (though there are serious objections to the restriction of the name of temperance to the restraint which is exercised with reference to the one indulgence of strong drink),—it is in the matter of so-called temperance that the principle of which we are speaking has grown most familiar. And there is a quiet beauty which I think nobody can help feeling in the fact that there are thousands of people in England and America to-day who are unostentatiously restricting or refusing themselves in an indulgence which they more or less desire, and which they know would be for them wholly innocent, lest they should do harm to the lives and characters of any of their brethren. There is a moral beauty in such a voluntary act which, in its small degree, is of the same kind with the sacrifice of Christ. Only we always must remember that the beauty of such an act is in its voluntariness, and that to make such relinquishment obligatory either by statute law or social edict is to rob it of its essential character. The beauty of it is gone so soon as the relinquishment becomes not a man's willing surrender of what he might retain, but the forced yielding of that which a state law or the despotism of a public opinion has forbidden.

And in the same principle we see what necessary and impassable limits there are to the moral power of any prohibitory legislation. It may be very necessary; it often is; but they who urge it most ought to feel deeply that it is always superficial and always temporary. With regard to all things not essentially and necessarily wrong, with regard to all things which a man has a right to do until some higher obligation comes in to control his right, you stand on no sure ground till you have brought your fellow-men to self-control. All saying to a man, "You shall not do that," is of little use unless it is leading on to a time when he shall say of himself, "I will not do that. I might do it if I would, but I will not do it. I have a right to do it, but I have no right to use my right."

You see how voluntariness lies at the root of it all. It is in the power which was in us to be something else that the moral beauty of being any good thing which we are resides. There is a beautiful life conceivable which should have been made involuntarily—by a compulsion which it could not have resisted—obedient and perfectly harmonious to the eternal goodness. Such a life would be indeed beautiful: a thing for men and angels to admire; a thing for God to look down on with delight as the sun looks down upon its own image in a crystal lake. But its beauty would not be moral beauty. Its beauty would be like the beauty of a strain of music or the beauty of a statue—not the true beauty of a character, not the beauty of a man; for there can be no true beauty of character where there is not voluntariness. We talk about the glory of resignation to the inevitable; and it is glorious. To stand with a smile upon your face at a stake to which you are chained, and from which you cannot get away, that is heroic. But the true glory is in resignation to the evitable. To stand unchained, with perfect power to go away, with perfect certainty that no man would drive you back—to stand held only by the invisible chains of higher duty, and, so standing, to let the fire creep up to the heart—that is the truer heroism. And there are men and women whom we meet every day in the streets, by whose side we sit every Sunday in our pews, who are doing that. Men call them fools. No man would blame them; many men would praise them if any day they gave up the self-imposed duty of their life and went through the gate that stands wide open into the unrestrained enjoyment of life. If the mother stopped being a slave to her ungrateful son, if the merchant let go the hopeless struggle to pay his honest debts, if the brother shook off his shoulders the weight of his worthless brother's life and sprang forward to the honours that seem to be within his grasp, there is no voice that would say a word of blame. The world of successful men would welcome with a shout this wise man who at last had broken through the hedge which had been shutting him up to failure and set himself free to take his rights. But what would the man's soul say to itself about it all? Would any success make up for the concession with which the man had won it? Would not the brightest fields of his new prosperity be haunted by the cry with which that hapless worthless brother sank into the waves when he shook him off as he struggled toward this golden shore? He has claimed his right to success; and everybody except himself owns that he had a right to claim it; but he himself knows that it was a right which he had no right to claim.

Oh, my dear friends, you know little of life if you do not know that there is always a sadness at the heart of every success. To have done anything in the way which men choose to call successful must always bring revelations of how imperfectly it has been done. Men who have watched your climbing send their cheers up to you as if you were standing on the summit; but you, from where you stand, can see how, peak beyond peak, the mountain range stretches away from you into the clouds. To succeed is always sad; but to succeed by the casting away of any of the chances of goodness and of useful work which God offered us, not merely to find that we have not reached the mountain's top, but to have climbed to where we are only by casting off the bundles of responsibility that God gave us to carry, that is beyond all things wretched.

I always like to trace how the laws which apply to action apply also to thought. Let me remind you very briefly of the way in which there are voluntary surrenders of mental comfort and peace which the truest minds often are ready to make, and out of which, if they make them, there comes in the end a richer and completer wisdom. A man deliberately turns his face to the hard problems of the universe. "If God is good, what means this world full of pain?" "If Christ has saved the world, why all this endless uproar and strife of sin?" "If God is light, why are His children walking in darkness?" "How could God have made men who He knew would be wicked?" "What is the future of the souls that obstinately sin?" You ask yourselves these questions; you carry them about upon your heart. Of course, in all the pews around you there are people enough, good friends of yours, who say to you, "Why need you think about those things? Are you not safe? Are you not sure of happiness? You have a right to peace, rest, comfort, the assurance of entire faith; take it, and do not worry over questions which are too high or too deep." But all your heart responds, "I cannot rest; I must know all I can know;" and so you deliberately give up the peace of unquestioning repose and go out into the sea where the questions cross and recross, and beat one another like the beating of the waves.

And now, what shall we say about all this—this voluntary surrender of that which is legitimately ours, because of some higher duty which can only be done in and by such renunciation? What can we say but this: it is the law of God, that wherever there is duty there is also possible joy. Just as the man who sees foliage knows that somewhere there must be water, although his eyes or ears cannot discern it, and the trees seem to grow out of the sand; so the man who is sure that in any spot there is duty for him to do knows that there is a happiness for him somewhere in the doing of that duty, even though for the present it seems to be a dreadful drudgery. In the expectation of that joy he works. The expectation of joy is joy; and so the man who in his voluntariness surrenders some delight or privilege, finds that there is a subtler mastery of happiness which is to be gained only by giving it up and seeking something higher, though for the time it seems to separate us from the happiness we love. Many and many an experience there is in this world which gives us the right to believe that happiness is something very coy and wilful, which, when we chase it, runs away from us; but, when we turn away from it and seek for something better, and forget to seek it, changes its mind and chases us. You remember, perhaps, in Tennyson's *Enoch Arden*—which whole poem, indeed, is a picture of the truth which I have tried to state to-night— how, when Enoch has made his resolution and deliberately determined that he will not claim the home to which he has a right, and has settled down to his solitary life, these lines describe his condition:—

> "He was not all unhappy. His resolve
> Upbore him, and firm faith, and evermore
> Prayer from a living source within the will,
> And beating up thro' all the bitter world,
> Like fountains of sweet water in the sea,
> Kept him a living soul."

What are such words as these but an echo of the strong words of Jesus, which declared that if a man lost his life for the highest purposes, "for my sake and the gospel's," he should find it. Indeed there are various half-mystic words of Christ which explain and illuminate this truth, of which our own experience bears witness, that when a man voluntarily surrenders that which is legitimately his for some sublimer claim, he does not really lose it; its spiritual essence, its precious soul, remains with him, and is still his. Think of these words in which the Lord described the recompense of those who abandoned everything for His sake— "There is no man that hath left house, or brethren, or sisters, or father, or mother, or wife, or children, or lands, for my sake, and the gospel's, but he shall receive an hundredfold now in this time, houses, and brethren, and sisters, and mothers, and children, and lands, with persecutions ; and in the world to come eternal life." The thing he gives away, that very thing, in its real substance, in its true value, he shall have.

Shall we not think that Christ spoke all His deep words out of His own experience. He Himself had known what it was to gain the life He lost, to have the thing that He surrendered. When He gave up the home of the foxes and the birds, it was to find a home all the more deeply in His Father's love. When he refused to call the angels to His help, the strength which was the meaning of the angels was surely entering into Him, and making Him ready for the battle which He was just about to fight.

This, then, is the sum of the whole matter. There will come to every manly man times in his life when he will see that there is something which is legitimately his, something which he has a right to, something which nobody can blame him if he takes and enjoys to the fullest, and yet something by whose voluntary and uncompelled surrender he can help his fellow-man and aid the work of Christ, and make the world better. Then will come that man's trial. If he fails, and cannot make the sacrifice, nobody will blame him ; he will simply sink into the great multitude of honourable, respectable, self-indulgent people who take the comfortable things which everybody owns that they are entitled to, and live their easy life without a question. But if he is of better stuff, and makes the renunciation of comfort for a higher work, then he goes up and stands—humbly, but really—with Jesus Christ. He enters into that other range, that other sort of life, where Jesus Christ lived. He is perfectly satisfied with that higher life. He does not envy, he does not grudge, the self-indulgent lives which he has left behind. He does not count up what he has lost; he does not ask whether he is happier or less happy than he would have been if he had kept what everybody says he had a right to keep. It is not a question of happiness with him at all; but gradually, without his seeking it or asking anything about it, he finds that the soul of the happiness which he has left behind is in him still. Like fountains of sweet water in the sea, it rises up and keeps him a living soul. He has left the world's pleasures and its privileges only to draw nearer to its necessities, which are its real life. So what he gave he keeps, a thousandfold even in this present time, and eternity is all before him, in the end everlasting life.

If there is any young life here which wants to be its best, let it be ready, not to throw away its privileges in cynical contempt of them, but to let any of them go when God reveals to it some purpose of a noble service, or an exalted suffering in which He may have made it possible for that young life to follow in the footsteps and to carry on the work of Christ.

XII.

GAMALIEL.[1]

"Gamaliel, a doctor of the law, had in reputation among all the people."—ACTS v. 34.

IT is strange how a single name here and there out of the great multitude of perished and forgotten names secures remembrance. It is almost as when one stands upon the seashore and looks out across the sea, and here and there upon the surface of the great ocean, all gray and monotonous, there comes one flash of silver; one single wave all by itself leaps up as if it were alive, and burns with a lustre which compels the eye to look at it. You ask yourself why that especial wave should have such peculiar privilege, and there is only one answer you can give. It is not any larger wave than the rest, and it is made of no different water from them; it is simply that that wave happened to leap just where the sun was smiting, and so the

[1] Preached at the Temple Church, London, Sunday morning, 1st July 1883.

sun smote it, and it became illustrious. So it is with the illustrious men. The sun of history shines on this great sea of human life; and the special career which happens to leap just where the sun is striking catches his glory and seizes men's notice and remembrance. If the man's life is larger than other lives, so much the better,—it catches so much more of sunshine. If it is of special fineness, made of more lustrous stuff than other men's, so much the better still,—it turns the sunshine into a peculiar radiance. But still the essential thing is that it should leap at the right moment and should be turned the right way. With those conditions even a very common life becomes illustrious; and without them the largest and the finest character melts back into the bosom of the humanity out of which it sprung, unknown, unnoticed, unremembered.

These illustrious men when they appear are, as would follow from what I have been saying, of more than merely exceptional, phenomenal value. In their illumination the whole great mass of humanity finds its illustration and understands itself. This is true in the most general aspect of them. And when we come to look at them in their more personal characteristics, each of them becomes the representative of some smaller group of humankind, to which he almost gives his name

Other men recognise themselves in these illuminated exhibitions of their qualities. They understand themselves better, and they are able better to declare the meaning of their lives to the world in the light of these their representatives.

There is always something interesting in seeing men thus realise themselves in the sight of the representative historic expressions of their characters. Often, indeed, it is only a degenerate caricature of the higher nature which they present. The dogmatist names himself by the great name of St. Paul, and thinks that his narrow dogmatism is of the same sort with the apostle's large-minded faith. The feeble sentimentalist counts himself the twin-brother of St. John. The dainty sceptic, dabbling in unbelief, takes the name of earnest, puzzled, simple-souled St. Thomas to himself. But, after all, there is a constant tendency in their association with the highest types of their several natures and tendencies to draw them upward and to make each of them a more worthy expression of his characteristic qualities than he could be if he knew it only in himself. In this truth lies one of the greatest advantages of the study of the representative men of human history.

I ask you to turn with me this morning to the story of a man whose name flashes for a moment as the light of the New Testament history falls upon the life of Jerusalem at the beginning of the Christian Church. The flash is only for a moment, and yet the impression which it leaves is very clear. Gamaliel is peculiarly a representative man, and the nature which he represents is one which appeals peculiarly to our modern life.

Let us recall his history. He was one of the most famous teachers of the Jewish law at Jerusalem in the days of Christ and in the years which immediately followed Christ's departure. It is not only from the New Testament that we know about him; all of the Jewish history of those days declares that he was one of the ablest and most famous of the learned men of the nation. He was the grandson of the great scholar and teacher Hillel, and he belonged distinctly to the same liberal school as his great ancestor. In those days there were two schools or parties among the orthodox religious Jews— the school of Shammai, which was strict and narrow; and the school of Hillel, which was liberal and free. Gamaliel was of the school of Hillel; he was a liberal Pharisee; he was of the same kind of men with Nicodemus and Joseph of Arimathea, who appear in the gospels as both Pharisees and Liberals. Gamaliel was one of the few rabbis who allowed their students the study of the literature of the Greeks. He taught that soldiers in war-time, and all persons engaged in works of mercy, duty, or necessity, should be exempt from the more stringent sabbatical traditions; he bade his disciples greet even the pagans on their feast-days with the "Peace be with you." In ways like these he showed the largeness of his spirit, and the people loved him. He was one of the seven among the Jewish doctors who alone have been honoured with the supreme title of Rabban. He lived to a good old age, and died about sixty years after the birth of Christ.

In the New Testament, Gamaliel appears twice, and both times in the most interesting way. First, he is the teacher of St. Paul, and so we are constantly led to speculate as to what part of the training of his great pupil's character is due to him; and in the second place, when the apostles were arrested very soon after the Pentecost for preaching Christ in Jerusalem, Gamaliel, a member of the Sanhedrim, before which they were brought for trial, uttered a memorable plea for toleration and delay of judgment. His words on that occasion are among the classic words of fairness and candour. He bids the hot-headed Jewish counsellors beware; he reminds them of how agitators before this have risen and soon come to nothing. "And now," he goes on, "I say unto you, refrain from these men, and let them alone: for if this counsel or this work be of men, it will come to nought: but if it be of God, ye cannot overthrow it; lest haply ye be found even to fight against God." And his words had their effect, and the disciples were released.

In the light of all these facts about him, and especially in view of these last-quoted words of his, it is not hard to see what sort of man Gamaliel was. He was, in the first place, both a great teacher and also a great preacher of toleration. These two qualities unite in him as the book of Acts shows him to us. And they are two qualities which ought always to unite. Every great teacher, every great scholar, ought to be aware of the mystery and of the mightiness of truth, and therefore he ought to be prepared to see truth linger and hesitate and seem to be retarded, and even seem to be turned back, and yet to keep a clear assurance that truth must come right in the end, and that the only way to help her is to keep her free, so that she shall be at liberty to help herself. There is something in Gamaliel which always reminds one of Milton, the great scholar and the great champion of toleration of the Puritan days. Gamaliel seems to feel what Milton feels so strongly, that any attempt to help truth save by securing her liberty is impertinent; that all attempts to make truth strong either by disarming her enemies or by choosing for her what weapons she shall fight her battles with, is not a homage to her strength, but an insulting insinuation of her weakness. The scholar of truth must trust truth ; that is Gamaliel's ground. The man of mere affairs may be a bigot, but not the scholar ; the student must claim for himself and for all men, liberty.

How true this is. You may insist if you will that you have found not merely the best but the only true way of conducting business or of managing the affairs of State. You may, if you have the power, compel the business of the market or the government of the country to be conducted in your special way. Sometimes, and to some extent always, such arbitrary selection of methods is necessary in practical affairs. And the vital forces of commerce and the State will work on, even if they do not work at their best, under whatever special form you may have chosen. But if you limit the search after truth, and forbid men anywhere, in any way, to seek knowledge, you paralyse the vital force of truth itself. He who is seeking anywhere for truth loses the true spirit of his search if he forbids any other man to seek for truth anywhere else. That is what makes bigotry so disastrous to the bigot.

Gamaliel, then, is the man of wise and generous

toleration. And this character, as I have said, has close connection with the fact that he was a teacher, the teacher of St. Paul. The world will always be most interested in him as the teacher of the greatest teacher, after Christ, of Christendom. In the picture of Christian history this Hebrew teacher finds a place, mainly because the future teacher of Christendom is sitting at his feet. He is, then, the broad-minded teacher, the man who earnestly inculcates his own views of truth, and at the same time knows and freely owns that truth is larger than his view. Such a teacher as that—such a man as that giving his life to teaching always has a special interest. He is one of those men who give other men the chance to make history rather than make it themselves. They themselves are almost of necessity relegated to obscurity. The very splendour of the career of their pupils, of which they are the creating cause, makes it impossible for the world to see them; as the flash of fire from the gun's mouth, and the rush of the burning shell on its tremendous way, makes it impossible to see the gun itself in whose deep heart the power of the explosion was conceived and born. It is evident that in this thought there lies a satisfaction which has been quite sufficient for many a noble mind. Many a great teacher has been perfectly satisfied with teachership, perfectly content to furnish the materials and conditions of effective and conspicuous activity to other minds, and to rest himself in obscurity as they went forth to prominence. We can picture to ourselves Gamaliel watching Paul. Sometimes approvingly, sometimes condemningly, we can think of the calm large-minded teacher following the career of his fiery-hearted scholar, and, however he disagreed with what he thought his delusions, rejoicing in his faithfulness and force. Always the teacher thus watching the pupil, who carries forth his teaching in new ways, is a most interesting sight, not without pathos.

And, if we look the other way, there are few things finer than to see the reverence and gratitude with which the best men of active life look back to the quiet teachers who furnished them with the materials of living. One of the most interesting things about many of our greatest statesmen has been their love and honour for their schoolmasters and college tutors. Even from the midst of his missionary journeys, even from his prison in Rome, we are able to believe that St. Paul looked back to the lessons of faithfulness and generosity which he had learned of the great teacher of his youth, and could see them still, though with a lustre grown faint and pale, even through the great light which had shone around him by Damascus, and the glory of the vision of the third heaven.

There are some of us whose work in life seems to assume mainly this character. Parents, teachers, quiet helpers of other lives, it seems as if we were rather providing other souls with the conditions of living than living ourselves. Indeed there are none of us whose lives in some of their aspects do not assume that look. It is good to know that he who makes nobler life possible by any conscious work of his for other people, therein lives nobly himself, not merely in their lives but in his own. Let us always remember that the perfect life was content as one of its highest titles to be called a teacher's life. In the apparent stationariness of much of our experience, seeing life flow by us, as the river flows by the tree, it is good to live thus by the life to which we try to minister, as the tree lives by the river whose waters it at the same time does something to colour and to direct.

But there is a larger view of Gamaliel than this. He has his relation not merely to St. Paul, but to the whole opening history of Christianity. I have quoted his words at the Sanhedrim when the apostles were on trial: "If this counsel or this work be of men, it will come to nought: but if it be of God, ye cannot overthrow it;" therefore, " refrain from these men, and let them alone."

There are some men whose whole influence is to keep history open, so that whatever good thing is trying to get done in the world can get done; not the doers of great things, but the men who help to keep the world so truly poised that good forces shall have a chance to work. These words of Gamaliel seem to point him out as being such a man. There are men who seem to shut up a community, so that, as far as their influence extends, if a new thought were waiting to be spoken or a new deed all ready to be done, it would be thrown back and made hopeless. Was not this exactly what Jesus charged upon the Scribes and Pharisees: "Ye shut up the kingdom of heaven against men. Ye neither go in yourselves; neither suffer ye them that are entering to go in"? It was not their special persecutions of enterprising and original people, not their special opposition to His immediate teaching, of which He was speaking then; it was rather the effect which all their life and spirit had upon the world. They made great deeds, fresh thoughts, enthusiastic consecration to first principles appear impossible. There is a still stronger instance of the same blighting power in what St. Mark says of the possibility of Jesus working His miracles in His own country: He "could there do no mighty work, because of the people's unbelief." It was possible for men so to shut up a whole district of the land that even Christ's marvellous power could not do its work there. And this is something which we can surely understand. In our own little circles are there not men so distrustful of the higher impulses, men in the largest and deepest sense so unbelieving and so scornful, that we see the young people, the earnest people, the fresh enthusiastic people, shut up their lives before them as the flowers shut up at night; and there is no hope for any great thing to be done or thought while they are there. I do not mean the sober, thoughtful, accurate, critical men and women who insist on submitting every impulsive thought and plan to a careful examination. They are not the murderers of enthusiasm; they kill no impulse except the silliest and most superficial. They are like the healthy frost, which kills the gnats and mosquitoes, but makes every higher being live with a fuller life. The men I speak of are men who are set upon making all the world live in their way, and who have no real faith in God, and therefore no real faith in man. Human force and goodness seem to them to be not vital growths with real life in them, but skilfully-arranged devices all artificially planned and pinned together, where if you altered the place of any single pin the whole must fall. Such men must blight the possibilities of any community they live in. But there are other men who, not doing themselves perhaps great deeds, seem to make great deeds, or at least to make great life, possible. Such men in our community, in our family circles, in our own little groups, whatever they are, any of us may be—men who shall do something to hold the soul of our little group in such expectancy and readiness, in such unwillingness to settle down upon the imperfect present as a finality, that when the inspired word or deed shall come, as it is sure to come some time, it shall find the atmosphere ready to receive it and transmit it. We cannot make the wind to blow, —it bloweth where it listeth; but we can keep the windows open, so that when it blows the chambered life about us shall not fail to receive its freshness.

If I am right in thinking that Gamaliel was a good type of this kind of man who keeps the world open for what God has to give to it, then it will certainly be well for us to study him more closely, and especially to look at this typical speech of his to see what we can of where this kind of power lies. I must quote it to you once again. "If this counsel or this work be of men, it will come to nought," he said; "but if it be of God, ye cannot overthrow it." The first thing that is evident about that speech is that the man who makes it believes in God; not a mere faith about God; he believes in God. To him evidently surrounding all that man does—behind it and before it and working through it—there is God. And with God are the final issues and destinies of things. Work as man will, he cannot make a plan succeed which God disowns; work as man will, he cannot make a plan fail which God approves. That is a noble and distinct faith. It is stepping across the line between fear and courage, between restlessness and peace, between intolerance and charity, when a man thoroughly, heartily, enthusiastically enters into that faith, when he comes to really believe that with all his heart and soul. These words of Gamaliel are the words of all really progressive spirits. They were the words of Martin Luther, who opened Europe and made the best of modern history a possibility. Fitly do they stand to-day carved upon the pedestal of his great statue at Wittenberg.

And yet we want to know what it is to believe in God and to trust Him for the great results of things. It is not to rest in idleness. Luther worked; Gamaliel worked. Nobody can doubt that Gamaliel went back from the Sanhedrim meeting to teach with all his might that Christianity was wrong. He had his thoughts, and he upheld them. He said, " This is the truth ;" only, as he said that, he must have said also to his scholars —young Saul of Tarsus sitting there among them —" There are some men here in Jerusalem—earnest, brave, enthusiastic, wofully deluded, as I think—who are asserting that not this which I tell you about the Messias, but something else quite the opposite is true. They are asserting that the Christ has come, and that His reign has begun. I think these men are wrong. I give you my reasons. By and by you will see their fanaticism wither and dry up because no life of God is in it. But now let them alone. Believe your truth, assert it, prove it, live it : so will you do your best to kill this folly." That was Gamaliel. That is the true spirit always. To hold your truth, to believe it with all your heart, to work with all your might first to make it real to yourself and then to show its preciousness to other men, and then—not till then, but then—to leave the questions of when and how and by whom it shall prevail, to God ; that is the true life of the true believer. There is no feeble unconcern and indiscriminateness there, and neither is there any excited hatred of the creed, the doctrine, or the Church which you think wholly wrong. You have not fled out of the furnace of bigotry only to freeze on the open and desolate plains of indifference. You believe, and yet you have no wish to persecute ; and any reader of the history of faith—nay, any student of his own soul—knows how rarely these two conditions have met in perfect harmony.

When I say that word "persecute," I dare say that I suggest the question which has been all the time upon some of your minds. Persecution sounds like a bygone word—a word of Gamaliel's time but not of ours. And no doubt in its worst forms in the best parts of the earth persecution has quite passed away. The stake and the scaffold for opinion's sake have disappeared in all enlightened lands. And yet all persecution did not pass away with them. There are far keener ways in which man may inflict pain on his fellow-man than by the axe or halter. Social disgrace and ostracism for the sake of one's belief come in to take the place of the more crude and violent punishments of other days. It may be said, perhaps, that these too are gone ; and in great part they are. No man to-day with any sort of manly earnestness about his creed could mind, it would seem, for a moment the petty indications of dislike and unpopularity which his creed might incur. The form in which persecution lingers still is one yet more subtle. It is in the disposition to attach disastrous consequences in this world or the next to honest opinions which we hold to be mistaken ; the desire to fasten upon intellectual convictions those stigmas of wickedness which can belong only to personal character, to call a man a bad man, and to make him, if we can, tremble at some future which we vaguely hold before him, who—just as honest and as faithful in the search for truth as we are—has seen truth differently from the way in which it has appeared to us. When that last form of terrorism shall have passed away—when we shall frankly own that there is nothing for which God in any world will punish any of His children except sin—then persecution will have finally perished. That day will come, partly by the advancement of man's own standards, by his willing acceptance of the better way, but partly also by the acceptance of a more and more clearly perceived necessity. Man will cease persecuting his brother man, partly because he will outgrow the wish to persecute, but partly also because he will see how useless it is to persecute; always our necessities come thus to reinforce our feeble sense of duty. We shall come in the end to welcome all the honest and earnest thought of men, partly because we see the good of it, however it differs from our own, and partly because we cannot help ourselves. In history it is by the combined forces of these two causes that every great progress of human thought has taken place.

And when all persecution goes, when the last effort to enforce opinion by any form of terror disappears, no doubt one of the greatest of all the blessings which its departure brings will be that there will come a chance and a demand for the two forms of human influence which will then have all the work to do. The greatest blessing of getting rid of the weeds is that the flowers can grow. Reason and life, these are the real forces which man always has a right to use to impress his belief upon his fellow-man. When you have thoroughly learned and thoroughly believed that it is both wrong and useless to try to frighten your fellow-man out of his faith into yours, then what remains? First, you may argue with him, tell him why you believe, show him how unreasonable his unbelief or his fanaticism is. That is legitimate, and it is good for any man or any creed when it is driven out of the dark ways of persecution and made to stand up fairly in the light and face the adversary in fair battle. And if you cannot argue, if your grounds for your belief, true as you know they are, are such as you cannot put forth in convincing words, or if the friend whom you want to convince is one to whose mind stated arguments bring no conviction, then there is only one thing left—you must live your faith. Oh, how often we have seen it! A true soul cannot, and will not, force its faith upon another soul. It hates, and it despairs of persecution. And it says (how often we have heard it!), " I cannot argue. I always make the better reason seem the worst, and dishonour the cause for which I plead. Am I not helpless!" And then just going on, hopeless of influencing others, just trying to live out its own life, to turn its own assured belief into obedient action, gradually other people have become aware, even if it has never discovered the fact itself, that this true soul was bearing a witness to truth which must have power. Not all men are capable of arguing or of receiving argument; but all men are capable of living and of appreciating life. In a live State the soldiers have their useful duty, but it is not the fighting soldiers who make the State's true strength or are its real defenders. Its faithful citizens, living their industrious lives within its institutions, which their lives are always filling with life, they are the true defenders of the State, making it strong, and making its strength impressively manifest to all the world. So the great faith needs learned reasoners; it cannot do without them. But it needs obedient servants and disciples more. And he who cannot argue, and will not persecute, may still know that his life is not useless for his faith. He may just live faithfully and leave the whole result to God, whose the faith really is if it is true.

And that brings us back once more to Gamaliel. Was he, then, right? Could he then, can a man to-day, leave all to God and be quietly sure that He will vindicate the truth? A thousand fluctuations in the varying battle make us doubt. Many and many a time it seems as if between the error and the truth it were merely a question of which had the cleverest men upon its side. And yet we know that, if there be a God at all, Gamaliel was right. There cannot be a God, and yet that which is of Him have no stronger assurance than that which is of man and of the earth. There must be time, there must be patience; but the real final question of two trees is the question of their roots. That which is rooted in God must live. There is no hope or peace anywhere in the world if this is not true. Who cares which way the fickle wind is blowing at this minute if there be no purpose which stands behind and governs it, no One who holds the winds in his hands? But if there be, who will not labour bravely, trying to put himself into the current of the great purpose of the world; begging to be defeated if he mistakes the great purpose and is helping evil when he thinks that he is helping good; ready to wait and work through all delays; with infinite patience ready to see men blundering and going wrong; ready to help them if he can,—sure of one thing and only one, that in the end, through every hindrance and delay, God must do right?

The final glory of Gamaliel lies there. He believed that God was the only life of this world, that all which did not live in Him must die. We do not know whether Gamaliel ever became a Christian before he died, whether, in this life, he ever saw that the true light which these poor prisoners adored was true and gave himself to Christ. The legends say that he did. History seems to say that he did not. But at least we know that if we have rightly read his character and story, he made the Christian faith more possible for other men, and he must somewhere, sometime—if not here, then beyond—have come to the truth and to the Christ Himself. I wish that I could speak to the Gamaliels here to-day, men not Christians, but men who are earnest, thoughtful, tolerant, and sure of God, pure and sincere, and ready for the light which God shall show them. Be sure, so I would say to them, be sure that no man in this world can be earnest and sure of God without helping the world to faith, often to a faith clearer than his own, or without going on himself to a completer and completer faith, and certainly at last somewhere coming to the perfect faith himself. Therefore be earnest and keep sure of God! Be earnest and keep sure of God! We who believe in Christ dare to be confident and say that we know that to every such soul the Way, the Truth, the Life must show Himself at last!

XIII.

THE GIFT AND ITS RETURN.[1]

"For with what measure ye mete, it shall be measured to you again."—MATTHEW vii. 2.

THE New Testament is full of the idea of a natural and necessary reciprocity between man and the things by which he is surrounded. "Whatsoever a man soweth that shall he also reap," writes St. Paul to the Galatians. "He that soweth sparingly shall reap also sparingly, and he that soweth bountifully shall reap also bountifully." The world seems to be a great field in which every man drops his seed, and which gives back to every man, not just the same thing which he dropped there, any more than the brown earth holds up to you in the autumn the same black berry which you hid under its bosom in the spring, but something which has its true correspondence and proportion to the seed to which it

[1] Preached in St. Margaret's Church, Westminster, Sunday evening, 8th July 1883.

is the legitimate and natural reply. Every gift has its return, every act has its consequence, every call has its answer in this great live, alert world, where man stands central, and all things have their eyes on Him and their ears open to His voice.

And I think that what impresses a thoughtful reader of the New Testament most is the way in which this fact of the reciprocity between man and his surroundings is the very element in which all life goes on. It is not something artificially arranged; it is inherent in the very natures of man and of the world. They could not be what they are and this fact not be true. True, it is constantly spoken of as the issue and result of the will of God. The New Testament is personal always, and it is personal here. What the world gives us in answer to what we give to it is constantly spoken of as given to us by God. "Ask and you shall have;" "Seek and you shall find," says Jesus. "Forgive and you shall be forgiven;" "Judge not and you shall not be judged;" "Give and it shall be given unto you;" "He that confesseth Me before men, him will I also confess." Here it is the will of an observant God that sends the answer to the thing we do. But God, in the New Testament idea of Him, is not merely the arranger of certain correspondences, the adjuster of rewards and punishments ; He is the spiritual element in the embrace of which all our life and all our relationships are born and work. As a man grows in the sunshine, as two men meet and look into each other's eyes and catch one another's sympathy, and share one another's life in the midst of warm, soft, vital ether, which at once supplies the vitality of both of them, and also carries the trembling sound of their voices and the living pictures of their faces to each other's ears and eyes; so we develop our own life and relate our own life to other lives within God, if we may say so. And why should we not say so when it is just what Paul said to the Athenians, as he declared upon Mars' Hill, "In Him we live, and move, and have our being"? Therefore it is that what the world returns to any man in answer to the force which he lays out upon it, comes to him in God, comes to him from God, and may truly be taken as God's encouragement or God's warning. God's will is not something separable from the essential and necessary working of the fundamental laws of the world ; it is the element in which those laws work, and which decrees their character. Let us understand this fully, and then we shall not be confused to-night as we speak of the necessary replies which a man's surroundings always make to what he is and does ; we shall be able freely to hear in those replies at once the working of an essential law, and at the same time the utterances of the will of God.

The necessary replies which a man's surroundings make to what he is and does,—this is our subject for this evening. "With what measure ye mete, it shall be measured to you again." It is a law of vast extent and wonderful exactness. The world is far more orderly than we believe ; a deeper and a truer justice runs through it than we imagine. We all go about calling ourselves victims, discoursing on the cruel world, and wondering that it should treat us so, when really we are only meeting the rebound of our own lives. What we have been to things about us has made it necessary that they should be this to us. As we have given ourselves to them, so they have given themselves to us. This is the law I want to trace with you, only begging you again to keep your minds, as I speak, clear of any materialism which would think that in mere earth itself resides this power of just and discriminating reply. It is as we and all things exist together in the great embracing and pervading element of God that all things give themselves to us as we give ourselves to them. So all the phenomena of life are at the same time divine judgments if we are only wise enough to read them.

It would be possible to trace our law even in physical nature. Newton's great generalisation, which he called the "Third Law of Motion," was, that "action and reaction are always equal to each other;" and that law has been one of the most pregnant of all truths about the mystery of force, one of the brightest windows through which modern eyes have looked into the world of nature. It has shown the whole world throbbing with the responsiveness of part to part. It has made men know that no force could work without another force replying to it. Every pressure involves resistance, every blow is answered by a blow in return. It fills the universe with life. Nothing is passive and nothing is uncaused; life and causation run through the lowest and the highest things. The trees and the plants are ready to reply to the least or the mightiest touch. Still, as in the prophecy of Habakkuk, "The stone cries on the wall, and the beam out of the timber answers it." Still, as in the book of Job, "The morning stars sing together," in the great rhythm of action and reaction which pervades the earth.

But it is of man and his reactions that I want to speak, tracing them briefly from the lowest region to the highest. Where shall we begin? Even with man's relations to the material earth the law is true. What different things she is to

all of us, this earth we live in! Why is it that
one man laughs at another's view about the earth,
and thinks him mad because of some strange value
that he places on it? Three men stand in the
same field and look around them; and then they
all cry out together. One of them exclaims, How
rich! another cries, How strange! another cries,
How beautiful! and then the three divide the field
between them, and they build their houses there;
and in a year you come back and see what answer
the same earth has made to each of her three
questioners. They have all talked with the ground
on which they lived, and heard its answers. They
have all held out their several hands, and the same
ground has put its own gift into each of them.
What have they got to show you? One cries,
"Come here and see my barn;" another cries,
"Come here and see my museum;" the other says,
"Let me read you my poem." That is a picture
of the way in which a generation or the race takes
the great earth and makes it different things to all
its children. With what measure we mete to it,
it measures to us again. This is the rebound of
the hard earth—sensitive and soft, although we call
it hard, and feeling with an instant keen discrimi-
nation the different touch of each different human
nature which is laid upon it. Reaction is equal
to action. Some of you may remember how our

New England poets' poet sings to the farmer over whose fields he has been wandering :—

> "One harvest from thy field
> Homeward brought the oxen strong;
> A second crop thine acres yield,
> Which I gather in a song."

This is what makes the everlasting interest of nature ; her capacity of endless association with man, from whom all real interest in the world must radiate, and to whom it always must return. As Emerson sings again of those whom he had loved, and who made the landscape in the midst of which he had loved them for ever dear :—

> "They took this valley for their toy,
> They played with it in every mood;
> A cell for prayer, a hall for joy,—
> They treated nature as they would.
>
> "They coloured the horizon round ;
> Stars flamed and faded as they bade ;
> All echoes hearkened for their sound,—
> They made the woodlands glad or mad."

"They treated nature as they would." So all men, all races, treat nature according to their wills, whether their wills be the deep utterances of their characters or only the light and fickle impulses of self-indulgence. And what they are to nature, nature is to them—to one man the siren, who fascinates him to drunkenness and death; to another, the wise friend, who teaches him all lessons of self-restraint and sobriety and patient hope and work.

But, after all, our relations to the world of nature are little more than illustrations of our relations to the world of men. With them our true relations are; and so let us pass on and see how true the law which we are looking at is there. I think that all of us come to feel very strongly, as we grow older, that what we get from fellow-men in all these close and pressing contacts into which life brings us with one another depends not nearly so much upon what the men are whom we touch, as upon what sort of men we are who touch them; and so, as we grow older, we ought to grow more careless about where we live, just in proportion as we become careful about what we are. What does it mean, that one man cannot go among any kind of men, however base and low, without getting happiness and good; while another man cannot go into the midst of the noblest and sweetest company without bringing out misery and despair and sin? I think there grows in us a strong conviction with our growing years that for a man to get bad out of the world of fellow-men is not necessarily a disgrace to the world of fellow-men, but is certainly a disgrace to him. Here are Jesus

and Judas : both go and give themselves to the
Pharisees ; both stand in the Pharisees' presence
and hear what they have to say. To Jesus these
Pharisees give back in return every day a deeper
consciousness of His own wondrous nature, a de-
vouter consecration to His Father, and a more
earnest pity for them. To Judas they give only
blacker dreams of treason, a falser disregard of
friendship and loyalty and honour. Let the two
tell the story of the men whom they have been
among—the Pharisees, whom both of them have
touched. Both will declare the sin which they
have felt ; but Jesus will declare how those sinners
have helped Him to Himself, and given Him new
chance to glorify His Father ; Judas, with bitter
cowardice, will curse them for his ruin. Unroll
the centuries and come down to our own day.
Take two boys in a class at college ; two clerks in
a shop in town. It is not good when either of
them is made cynical, and sneers at the possibility
of virtue because of the vice which he has felt in
its contamination at his side. The true soul, with
a character of its own, will learn the possibility of
being good from his own consciousness, all the
more strongly because of the vice that touches him.
No soul, bad in itself, can really learn the possibility of goodness by mere sight and touch even
of a world of saints, and no soul really good can

T

lose the noble consciousness that man was made for goodness, even though all the world but him is steeped in wickedness,—nay, in subtle ways he will feed that consciousness there.

And so there is a perpetual qualification, an ever-recurring limitation to the truth of all that we can say about the influence of friendship. You hear men say to you, "Seek the society of noble men. Live with the true, the faithful, and the brave; so you shall be true and brave and faithful." It is most wise advice; it is the thing you ought to do; but if you think that that is all, if men talk to you as if that were all, and as if the working of that law were certain, you both are wrong. There are men enough in the world to-day who are being made worse by living with the best and purest. Judas could never have come to be the wretch he was if he had lived out his quiet stupid days among the men in Kerioth, and Jesus of Nazareth had never crossed his path. Many an unbeliever is being made more unbelieving by the faith which is filling the house he lives in. Many an impure heart is growing viler because of the purity with which it lives in daily company. Many a narrow soul is not broadened but narrowed, pinched into a more wretched selfishness, by the large thought and sweet charity which bathes it. Souls are darker for the sunshine, souls are colder for the warmth, with which they live in daily company. And why? Because heaven does not make holiness, but holiness makes heaven; because if you do not give yourself in sympathy to goodness, goodness cannot give itself in influence to you, because with what measure ye mete it shall be measured unto you.

I know that words like these may well create misgivings in the minds of some of you who hear them as you think over your experience. You have really given yourself to men; you know that you have given yourself sympathetically and unselfishly; and where is your return? Reaction has not equalled action; they have not given themselves to you; they have misunderstood you; they have shut their doors the closer the more you knocked. After years of devotion you stand alone among an unregardful, perhaps among a contemptuous worldful of fellow-men. But oh, my friend, do not think that the only way in which a man can give you of himself is by an honour and affection of which he is conscious and of which you are aware. Let me not think that I get nothing from the man who misunderstands all my attempts to serve him and who scorns me when I know that I deserve his sympathy. Love and respect are the wrappings in which men give their best gifts of character to one another. We learn to think of the gifts by their bright beautiful wrappings. The gifts are beautiful to us, in part because of the beautiful enfoldings in which they have come to us. But if some day a man thrusts into my hands the gift all naked and stripped of its natural legitimate adornments, shall I not take it? Shall I not see all the more the real essential beauty and preciousness that is in it just because the silk and silver which I looked for to proclaim its preciousness are swept away. Ah! it would be sad enough if only the men who understood us and were grateful to us when we gave ourselves to them, had help to give us in return! The good reformer whom you try to help in his reform, and who turns off from you contemptuously because he distrusts you, seeing that your ways are different from his, he does not make you happy—he makes you unhappy; but he makes you good, he leads you to a truer insight, a more profound unselfishness. And so (it is the old lesson), not until goodness becomes the one thing that you desire, not until you gauge all growth and gain by that, not until then can you really know that the law has worked, the promise has been fulfilled. With what measure you gave yourself to him, he has given himself—the heart of himself, which is not his favour, not his love, but his goodness, the real heart of himself to you.

For the rest you can easily wait until you both come to the better world, where misconceptions shall have passed away and the outward forms and envelopes of things shall correspond perfectly with their inner substances for ever.

This is the way in which good men give us their goodness if we really give ourselves unselfishly to them. And how is it if he to whom you give yourselves is not a good man but a bad man? How is it when the patient father devotes himself to a reckless child, or the long-suffering wife to the brutal husband? Who of us has not seen how the devoted life, even if it failed to develop the better life in the soul for which it sacrificed itself, and so did not win that soul as it longed to do for its reward, still drew for itself out of its labour for the degraded soul a new abundance of the very virtues which it could not plant in such reluctant soil. The pure nature may fail to make the wretch it loves pure, but it becomes more pure itself in the long struggle. The tender soul wins deeper tenderness in its despairing effort to soften the brutal soul beside it. The brave patriot cannot make the sluggish nation spring upon its feet for liberty, but his appeals summon a deeper patriotism and love of freedom in his own patriotic liberty-loving heart. Alas for us if we only gave to those who help us a return proportioned to our poor acceptance and appropriation of their help. It is not how we take them, but how they give themselves to us, that settles what shall be the rebound from us to their own lives. Often it is good to know that if the light that has shone upon us seems to have left us wholly dark, it has at least drawn out of our darkness some new, deeper, and finer brightness for him from whom it came.

So each man gets out of the world of men the rebound, the increase and development of what he brings there. Let us see how the same law applies to the truths which men believe, or the causes for which they labour. Every thoughtful observer sees two things, I think, about men's relations to their creeds and their occupations: first, that every creed or profession has a great influence upon the man who believes or practises it; and second, that no creed or occupation can ever give anything to a man except what his own nature brings a demand and fitness for. The first of these truths makes our creeds and occupations seem of vast importance; the second makes us know that of yet vaster moment is the personal character of the believer and the worker. Indeed, to speak first of our occupations, I think there is no more striking illustration of the working of the law of action and reaction than appears in what goes on between a man and the cause or profession to which his life is given. Nowhere is it so true that with what measure you mete it shall be measured to you again. You are a young man just in business, perhaps; you have heard a great deal, it may be, of the influences of business life upon a man. If you are at all reflective—if you care at all what happens to the inner part of you —you will begin by and by to look for the signs of the working of those influences of which you have heard upon yourself. You will be surprised to see that some of them come, and some of them fail to come entirely. It is impossible to say of you, "The influence of trade is this and this; therefore in time this new trader will be so and so." No doubt it is true in general, but in the particular case it will be yourself that decides what business is to make of you. Generous or stingy, large-idead or small-idead, appreciative or unappreciative of other occupations than your own; these things you will be, not invariably according to the kind of trade you are engaged in, but distinctively according to the kind of manhood which you put into your trade. So it is everywhere. Plenty of young men studying law, and coming out full of prejudice and the very essential spirit of injustice; plenty of young men studying medicine, and coming out coarse instead of fine, brutal instead of reverent; plenty of young men studying divinity, and gathering unspirituality and uncharitableness out of the very marrow of the gospel; plenty of men, old and young, giving their days and nights to philanthropy and the public weal, and growing more selfish and jealous out of the very substance of practical benevolence. Nay, shall we not say it? plenty of churchmen, earnest, true, devoted, who, bringing to the Church unchurchly hearts, hearts lacking in the breadth and simplicity and freedom and devotion of the true catholicity, are made unchurchly by all their Church associations, and come in the end to partisanship, which is the most unchurchly thing on earth.

And then see how it is with creeds. We try to bring one friend to hold some certain faith, certain that if he does hold it, it will influence his character; and we are right. Great is the power of truth! As he thinketh in his heart so is he! And yet behind this fact there always is the other, that no truth can give its treasure up to any man except through that in him which is conformable to it. A creed must fill a man's character before it really takes possession of his mind, as the ocean has to fill a vessel with its water before it can swallow it up into its depth. Take, for instance, the single truth of the Incarnation of Christ; that God has manifested Himself in intimate union with humanity. You love that truth and live by it. It gives you out of its heart stores of help and strength and comfort. Then you bring your child or your friend to it and say, " Believe this blessed truth and it shall help you too." He does believe it so far as arguments can make him, and it does not help him in the least. He gets out of it nothing. And by and by you begin to feel where the difficulty is. He brings to the intellectual conception no spiritual condition which can summon forth its virtue. He has no craving after higher company, no hungry need of God, no high perception of the possibility of man. No self, rich and at the same time needy with all these, does he give to the sublime truth of the Incarnation, and so it gives nothing back to him.

Happily the truth has a previous power to make men conscious of their need of it before it offers itself to them for their belief. So it is able, as all great truths are, first to create the spirituality which can believe it; as a great nature not merely offers itself to us to love and honour, but before that, lifts and refines us, so that we shall be capable of loving and honouring it. But until a creed has done that for a man, it cannot give him its real truth. The more he believes it, the more he may get out of it just exactly the opposite of its real sense and meaning. This is the reason why you cannot finally judge men by their creeds.

A man may hold the most spiritual doctrine, and be carnal and mercenary; a man may hold the broadest truth, and be a bigot; and, on the other hand, all our religious history bears witness that a man may hold hard, crude, narrow doctrine, and yet gather out of his belief in it rich, warm, sweet holiness which men and God must love. It does not prove, as men so often superficially and feebly say, that there is no value in the differences of doctrines; but it does keep always superior, always supreme, the greater value that is in the differences of men.

I turn to one more illustration of the working of our law—the highest, the completest of them all. A man gives himself to nature, he gives himself to the world and fellow-man, he gives himself to truth; and then, as the crown of all, as that which ought to come first and be the comprehending power of all the rest, he gives himself to Jesus. They are old and familiar words. They are words which have been precious to so many souls, words which have been held, as it were, in so many hands of all degrees of purity and earnestness, that it is no wonder if they come to us with some memory of the lowness and insincerity which has sometimes been laid upon them. Men have put many meanings into them. The exhorter in the inquiry meeting has assailed the soul of some anxious disciple, and questioned him, "Have you given yourself to Jesus?" and urged him, "Will you not give yourself to Jesus now?" until the act has seemed to be some strange external transaction which a man might do almost as he would draw money out of one bank and deposit it in another which was safer. All this has made the words seem misty sometimes, and unreal; but yet they are great words which we cannot, which the world never can, let go. There are no other words to take their place. They describe the completest action that the spiritual man can do. When a man most completely gathers up himself, his standards, his wishes, his resolutions, his loves, his plans, his powers, and transfers them all together to a new region where holiness shall be the law and love the motive of their life, there are no words to tell what that change is that are so comprehensive and complete as these, That man has given himself to Jesus. When I want to urge my friend to one entire salvation, in which all the partial salvations of conduct, of happiness, of taste shall be included, I can ask him nothing larger than this old question, which has summoned such multitudes of people to the higher life, and so which will be dear in their remembrance throughout all eternity—the question of questions, Will you not give yourself to Jesus?

And now, in that great giving, in that supreme

self-consecration, does our law still hold, the law of action and reaction, the law that only in the measure in which the gift is given can the answer come? Indeed it does. Nowhere, as all our experience bears witness, does it so completely hold. For there are different measures in which men give themselves to Christ, and Christ despises none of them; but in different measures He again is compelled to give Himself back to them. See how they come! One man approaches the divine Redeemer asking no divine redemption, but touched and fascinated by the beauty of that perfect life. He would feed his wonder, he would cultivate his taste, upon it. To him Jesus gives what he asks, and with delighted wonder and with cultivated taste the satisfied asker goes away. It is as if a man painted a mountain for its picturesqueness, and carried off his picture in delight, never dreaming that he left behind him in the mountain's bosom treasures of gold which only waited for his hand to gather them. Another man comes to Jesus with a self that is all alive with curiosity. He takes Christ's revelations—for Christ does not refuse him either—and goes away content to know much of God and man, and what there is beyond this world. Another man comes to Jesus with a self all trembling with fear, all eager for safety, and Jesus satisfies him; He lets him know that even the humblest, and most ignorant, and least aspiring soul, which repents of and forsakes its sin, and seeks forgiveness, shall not be lost. Each gets from Jesus that which the nature which He brings can take. With what measure each gives himself to the Saviour, the Saviour gives Himself in His salvation back to each. Only when at last there comes a man with his self all open, with door behind door, back into the most secret chambers, all unclosed, ready to give himself entirely, wanting everything, ready to take everything that Jesus has to give, wanting and ready to take the whole of Jesus into the whole of himself, only then are the last gates withdrawn ; and as when the ocean gathers itself up and enters with its tide the open mouth of the river, like a conqueror riding into a surrendered town, so does the Lord in all His richness, with His perfect standards, His mighty motives, His infinite hopes, give Himself to the soul which has been utterly given to Him.

Men talk as if it were not always so. Men talk as if because Christ is the same loving, willing Christ for all of us, and all of us are nothing and can have nothing but for Him, therefore the meagre mercenary saint ought to shine with the same lustre as the pure spirit passionate for holiness, and ready for all the completed will of God. As if one said that because the sun is the same sun always, and because there is no light except from Him, therefore the rose and the daisy ought to look alike. No! He in His love outgoes our prayers. He gives us more of what we ask than we know how to ask for; more beauty to the seeker after beauty, more wisdom to the student, more safety to the poor culprit asking forgiveness. And He is always trying to make the self which asks a larger self that He may give it other things of higher kinds. But yet the truth remains, that at each moment He can give Himself to us only as at that moment we give ourselves to Him. As when in some foreign land, in some strange shrine of Romish or Pagan religion, all glorious with art, all blazing with the light of precious stones, there bend around the altar the true devotees who believe with all their souls; while at the door, with heads uncovered and with faces solemnised by the presence of a ceremony in which they do not believe and in which they take no part, lingers a group of travellers full of joy at the wondrous beauty of the place; and as when the music ceases and the lights go out they go away, each carrying what it was in him to receive,—the devotee his spiritual peace, the artistic tourist his æsthetic joy: so men bestow themselves on Christ, and by the selves that they bestow on Him the giving of Himself to them must of necessity be measured.

I close in haste with what must be the necessary consequence of this. It is not enough that Christ should stand ready to give us His blessings. He must give us the nature to which those blessings can be given. What we want of Him is not merely His gifts; it is ourselves; He must give us them first. To them only can He give Himself, which is His perfect gift. Not merely with outstretched hands but with open hearts we must stand before Him. We must pray not merely that the kingdom of heaven may come, but that we may be born again, so that we may see it. If that prayer shall be answered, then to each of us even here upon the earth shall begin that which is to be the everlasting wonder and delight of heaven, the perfect giving of the Lord to souls that are perfectly given to Him, the everlasting action and reaction, the unhindered beating back and forth of need and grace between the Saviour on His throne and His servants at their tireless work for Him.

XIV.

"YOUR JOY NO MAN TAKETH FROM YOU."[1]

" And your joy no man taketh from you."—JOHN xvi. 22.

THAT our happiness is largely in the power of other people than ourselves is a conviction which we reach very early in our lives. Our joys seem to stand with open gates, so that almost any intruder may come in. The child whose life has not yet separated itself from the parent life, and still shares its fortunes; the merchant whose ship sails or founders with the great business fleet; the thinker who cannot escape the intellectual tendencies and imperfections of his times; the public man whose good name is in the keeping of the fickle populace—all of these are illustrations of the way in which the satisfaction and the peace of life are always open to invasion. No man can shut his gates and say, "I will find my happiness only

---

[1] Preached in Christ Church, Marylebone, London, Sunday morning, 15th July 1883.

in myself, and what I find no man shall take away from me." If any man says that he dooms himself to the most meagre life, and even in that he fails; even the poor fields which he can plant with his own seed he cannot keep completely to himself. It seems as if all our social arrangements and relationships were not more fitted to make us furnishers of joy to one another than they are to give to every man the chance to put his hand, if he wills, into the midst of some other man's lot, and to pluck away its happiness. Husband and wife, father and child, teacher and scholar, master and servant—how they all hold each other's pleasures at their will!

This is one view of life which is perpetually presenting itself. It stands up face to face with that other thought which all self-reliant and strong men try to keep hold of—the thought of self-sufficiency. To be independent of our fellow-men, to have the sources of all happiness in our own lives, to let the world swing and surge around us like the ocean around a steadfast rock—this is the other thought which no man can wholly cast away. It never finds its realisation; it always meets the interference of our brethren. Practically, almost all men's lives vacillate between the two. One moment we are all our own, keeping our own reserves, deciding our own destinies. The next moment we are all our neighbour's. He decides whether we are to be sad or happy, good or bad.

It is in the midst of a bewilderment like this that Christ comes in with the words which I have made my text this morning. As He sat with His disciples at the farewell supper, He looked around on them, and said, " I will see you again and your heart shall rejoice, and your joy no man taketh from you." In these words He declared that there was a joy which no man could disturb. There is a limit to our power over one another; there is a chamber of our inner selves where we may turn the key and no one can come in. I want to study that limit with you; I want to see whether we can discover where it runs and how it can be recognised. Where is it that, behind all the regions in which we are what other men make us, we can, we must be ourselves?

And first, the very fact that there is such a limit interests us. We can see how good it is for a man's life that, while there should be great regions of his happiness which are involved with what other men are and do, there should be also other regions which no man but himself can touch. The completest house for a man to live in is one whose outer rooms are hospitably open to whoever comes with any claim to hospitality, but which has inner chambers where only the master of the house and those who make up his household have a right to enter. The best stock of ideas which any man can keep is that which, while it is in the main harmonious with the thoughts of other men who live in the same time, and subject to their influence, yet has at its heart convictions which are the man's own, and which no other can invade. Now, is it not the same with regard to the happiness of life? There would be something almost terrible if each of us held his power of happiness untouched, untouchable by any other man. Think how much of the finest and richest of our intercourse with one another, how much of the most delicate consideration, how much of the purest motive for self-sacrifice and patience, would be lost if we had no power of invading and interfering with each other's joy. It would be almost a world of chartered selfishness. Why should I think of any one except myself if, no matter what I do, I cannot hurt that happiness which my brother carries shut away in the safe precincts of his own life? No. It is the pledge of our best intercourse with one another, the assurance of our sacredest relationships, that we have vast power to make one another unhappy. The necessary condition of that privilege which the father has of filling his child's life with sunshine is the other power, which just as certainly belongs to him, of darkening it with a heavy cloud. What would you care for any man's sympathy or approbation if all the while you knew that that same man's sneer or coldness would not give you even a twinge of pain? So necessary is it to our best life with one another that we should have power over one another's joy.

And yet we can see just as clearly how dreadful it would be if this power reached in to the deepest happinesses of which we are capable. All of us practically insist that there shall be some enjoyments with which no man shall interfere. With my ordinary acquaintances almost any man's slander may put me for the time out of conceit, but my friendship with my tried and trusted friend there is no slander that can ruffle for a moment. My light prejudices and tastes any zephyr may disturb, but upon my deep and satisfied convictions of what is true a tempest may blow in all its fury and they will not shake. Every deep and true man, every man with a genuine personal character, has some source of pleasure so hidden away that no man's foot can find it, no human malice can poison it. He himself must change before he can lose that enjoyment.

Now hear what Jesus says to His disciples— "Your heart shall rejoice and your joy no man taketh from you." It was a special joy, the inmost, the most secret and sacred of all joys which their Master promised. Not for those disciples more than for other men was nature to be changed, or their relations with their fellow-men to be robbed of the power of painfulness. Still, if you stabbed them they would bleed, if you burnt them they would smart. Still, if men taunted them they would quiver with the blow, if men were ungrateful to them their hearts sank in disappointment. Still, just as before Christ gave them His promise, their reverence was shocked, their love was wounded, their trust was betrayed, their motives were misjudged by fellow-men. But behind all this His words revealed to them a self out of men's power, something which no fellow-man could touch. As I think about their after lives, I can see them perpetually retreating into that, I can see them letting other joys go and not hating the hands which robbed them of them in the consciousness of this inmost joy, which no intrusion could invade. As I watch the growing life of the disciples, I see them coming to the best picture of what a human life ought to be, open and sensitive and sympathetic, and yet all the while self-respectful and independent; feeling other men and yet living their own life; as responsive as the ocean's surface to the winds of the living humanity which blew across them, and yet keeping, like the ocean, a calm and hidden depth which no storm upon the surface could disturb.

And Jesus tells His disciples just what the power of this secret joy is to be. It is to be His presence with them: "I will see you again, and your heart shall rejoice, and your joy no man taketh from you." Everything is based upon the association which they are to have with Christ their Master. There is nothing at all of self-sufficiency in what is promised. It is not that these men are to develop some interior strength, or to drift into some region of calm indifference where the influences of their fellow-men shall not touch them any longer. It is that they are to come to a new life with Him. The new joy which is to enter into them, which they are to enter into, is to be distinctly a joy of relationship and not of self-containment, a joy which is to escape the invasion of the men who disturb all other joys by being held in the hand of a stronger being out of which no earthly power shall be able to pluck it away.

And how natural this is! how it agrees with all that we know of the perpetual necessities of human nature! Only the association of some higher and stronger person can even really save one from the absorption and contamination of some lower persons who are swamping and ruining his life. Suppose you have a boy who is being overwhelmed and lost by and through his faculties of companionship. Have you not learned, all of you who are considerate and thoughtful parents, that it is through these same faculties of companionship that he must be saved? When I talk about his being lost and saved I mean what these words literally signify, and not what usage has attached to them as a sort of secondary meaning. A boy is lost when he ceases to be a positive and individual existence, when he becomes a mere puppet or echo or image of the lives around him. A boy is saved when his life is plucked out of the sea of imitation and promiscuous subserviency, and made a real thing, with its own consciousness, its own intentions, its own meaning, its own character. Suppose, in this sense, your boy's life is being lost, how will you save it? Can there be any power like that of a stronger person, a large, rich, simple nature, who, entering into close companionship with this flickering life, shall steady it, reveal it to itself, call out its best activities, and open for it a positive career. It must be a person who makes high demands, who declares duties, and who clothes those duties with the imperiousness of love. It will not be simply by forbidding your boy to have connection with those poor companions who are dissipating him; it will not be by shutting him in upon himself that you will save him. A stronger person must be his saviour; a life that shall control and lift his life must make him be himself. Now this is just what Jesus did for those disciples. He never once said to them, "Be yourselves." He said, "Be mine." And it was when He gave them His things to do, when He said to them, "Go preach," "Go heal," "Go build the Church," that through these channels of obedience He poured His life into their life, and gave to them a fresh and joyous being, far in behind the power of any man to touch or blight.

Some men who talk about the influence of Jesus seem to make it a mere sentimental thing. They dwell upon the love which He poured out upon His friends. They show us love glowing in the hearts and shining from the faces of those disciples in return. Other men talk about the mastery of Christ. He gave His servants things to do. He said, "Take up this cross," "Behold this task which waits for you." He shaped their lives into new habits. It was not either of these alone. Until we grasp them both into one thought we have not understood His power. He loved them and made them love Him, but it was through the obedience which He demanded of them that His love became a transforming power. That was His company with them, the fulness, the completeness of the idea of companionship. And He is just the same to us. To us too He brings love awakening love, and authority demanding obedience. " Lo, I am with you alway," He declares. And souls to-day, many and many of your souls, my friends, have found the rich fulfilment of His promise. Sometimes it comes to us with a strange surprise. When we are living on as if we lived alone, when we are sitting working silently in some still room which we think is empty but for our own presence, when we are busy in some work which seems as if it were our work, to be done as we should please ; slowly, sweetly, surely we become aware of a richer presence which is truly with us, of a love which enfolds us, and an authority which controls us. We are not alone. The work is not our work but His. The strength to do it with is not to be called up out of the depths of ourselves, but taken down from the heights of Him. The room is full, the world is full of Jesus. He is doing what he said he would do. He is with us as He said He would be ; and as we answer love with love and authority with obedience, we find that we are indeed lifted into a sober and serious happiness which nothing can invade, a joy which no man can take from us.

Let us try to bear this in mind as we pass on

now to speak of some of the interferences with the pleasures of life which come from our fellow-men, and of the way in which the soul's life with Christ puts those same pleasures out of the reach of any fellow-man's intrusion. Take first, if you please, the pleasure of energetic action. It is a joy which makes life bright to the best men; a joy so bright that never to have felt it, not to feel it always beating like the blood through all one's veins, must surely be a very desolate and dull existence. There are men who make their life out of idleness, out of having the world do for them what they need, and in such strange shapes are some men made, that no doubt there is for some men some sort of joy in that. But to be at work, to do things for the world, to turn the currents of the things about us by our will, to make our existence a positive element, even though it be no bigger than a grain of sand, in this great system where we live, that is a new joy of which the idle man knows no more than the mole knows of the sunshine, or the serpent of the eagle's triumphant flight into the upper air. The man who knows indeed what it is to act, to work, cries out, "This, this alone is to live!" Oh, the poor creatures whom their father's money or their own sluggish wills have robbed of the great human delight of action, the men to whom " things provided come without the sweet sense of providing." But what then? What are the interferences which this joy meets? Are they not these? I speak only of those which come from fellowmen, not of those which are the result of the hard nature of the material of the earth we have to work on. Are they not these? Some opposition to our action by the action of some other active man; or the contemptuous discovery and announcement of the incompleteness of the thing we do; or the ingratitude and irresponsiveness of the men whom we want our act to benefit. Opposition, criticism, and ingratitude, these are the ways in which other men meet an active man, and take the joy of his activity away from him, and make his work a drudgery. Here is a man in public life. The happiness of dealing with the state's affairs, of throwing his will and labour into the country's destinies, is what his soul is full of; he has dreamed of it while he was a boy, and now that he is a man all his manhood triumphs in it. Toil counts for nothing, fatigue and sleeplessness he never reckons as he pursues the joy of public life, of action on the destinies of men. But by and by what is it that has taken away his joy? Is it not these things which I described? Other men have stepped across his path, and thrown their will and energy into the face of his, and hindered him from doing what he meant to do. Other men have looked through what he has done and told the world and told him, what his heart knew only too well before, how far what he has done is from what it ought to be. Other men for whom he laboured have turned their backs on him and gone away, giving him curses instead of thanks. Opposition, criticism, and ingratitude, through these three gates other men's lives have crept in on him, and stolen away the joy of his life. Still he may work on from habit or from duty, but the joy of working is departed; it is a dreary drudgery; it is an hourly weariness. Oh, what hosts of active men there are who in their middle life still go on working, but with the spring all gone! The joy of work some man, some contact with the life of men, has taken from them.

Could that have been helped? Is there any help for that in all the world? If not, if all my joy in action is at the mercy of my fellow-men, it is a dreadful world to live and work in. I may keep on working in spite of them; they may not be able to prevent me from that; but if they can take the joy out of my work, it is a dreadful world. But now suppose that Christ had been with that man whom I described—Christ in His love and His authority—Christ the Friend and the Master. I mean it really. Suppose—for, oh, it is at least supposable — that behind every other motive, shining through every other motive which made the man work, there had been this, the love of Christ. Whoever else he worked for secondarily, he worked for Jesus first of all. Would that have made no difference? Like an electric atmosphere poured around the shrine in which a jewel rests, so that no hand can be thrust through to steal the jewel; so round the work, full of its joy, is poured the love of Christ, out of which no man can snatch it. Suppose that some strong opponent keeps him from doing what he wants to do,—there is still the assurance that his doing that is but a part of a vaster accomplishment, the will of his great Master, which he knows must come in its completeness whether this special act of his attain success or not.

Suppose that men taunt him with his action's incompleteness. If he is really serving Christ, it is not as a whole but as a part, it is as incomplete that he has counted his act of any value. The incompleteness of his action is absorbed and contained in the larger completeness of his Master. He need not be complete in Himself, held as his life is in the perfection of his Lord.

And yet again, suppose that men turn from Him with ingratitude. What then? If he has really been at work not for them ultimately, but for Christ, then their falling away may only leave the air more clear for him to hear that "Well done," which is the only praise he really values. Opposition and hindrance cannot pluck away his joy, for it is not his success but Christ's that he is seeking. Criticism cannot mar his happiness, for he has pretended to nothing,—all he has tried to do is to serve Christ. Ingratitude cannot make him wretched, for he appeals to Christ's truer judgment. To every consecrated labourer who works for Christ there is a joy in working which no man can take away from him.

Turn now and see how all this is true of Christian thought and the struggle after truth as well as Christian action. Thought and the struggle after truth are the best joys of the best men. To follow out the lines of speculation and of revelation until they lead us near the heart of things, which yet we know that we can never perfectly reach; to make some few steps forward on the journey which stretches out before us, endlessly tempting and interesting, into eternity; to add each day some new stone to the structure whose lines already as they leave the earth prophesy an infinite height for the far topstone,—he has not lived who has not felt this pleasure. He is not really living, however full he may be of warmth of feeling and of energy in action, who does not in some degree know what it is to crave ideas and knowledge, to seek for truth, and to delight in finding it.

Forgive me if I turn aside one moment from my course to say that the religious temper, while, in one action of it, it has always been the great inspirer of intellectual life, has always shown another tendency, to depreciate and deaden mental action, to be content with glowing feeling and with faithful action, as if they made up the whole life of the religious man. Against that tendency every man who is religious ought to be upon his guard. It would be a dreadful thing, it would almost prove that any form of religion was not divine—at least it would show that it had lost much of the beauty of its divine creation—if it did not recognise that man's best happiness demands the exercise of his mental powers, and so did not invite these powers to free and eager use.

But yet it seems to me that every thinking man discovers that the joy of thought, as delicate as it is fine and pure, is one that lies peculiarly within the power of our fellow-men. And why? It is not that our fellow-men may contradict and even contemptuously abuse some opinion which we hold as true. If we do really hold it perfectly as true, that is a little thing; it does not hurt us; it does not disturb the quiet happy confidence with which we rest our faith upon the well-proved certainty. But the trouble is that the more one thinks and studies, the more he becomes aware how infinite is truth. The truth which he has learned on any subject, he becomes aware, is not the whole. There is another side. There is a strange bewildering way in which just the opposite of the truth which he has learned is true. Every time, then, that any reasoner impugns our truth it starts up all this consciousness. We see how little of absolute impregnable certainty we have really reached. We see how far we are, even upon the subject which we know best, from having reached the end of things and laid our faith securely beside the ever green and solid shore to which the tides are struggling. Upon the subject which we know best we are still out at sea. Every time a fellow-man's finger touches our faith, it makes it rock, and compels us to feel that, however well anchored it is, so that it will not drift, it is very far from being morticed and bolted into the solid ground. This is the reason why so many people, when their faith is once attained, keep it not merely as a very precious but as a very frail and brittle thing. They will not talk with any one about it. They will not read anything upon the other side. They will keep out of the way of anything which for one moment can remind them that their faith is not complete, that they have not yet understood and settled everything concerning man and God. They stand guard over their peace in believing, not merely with an instinctive knowledge that the infidels and sceptics are trying to take it away from them, but with an instinctive fear lest they shall succeed in their attempt.

We know this is not good; and yet we very often do not see how it is to be escaped. The real escape, I think, lies here. The Christian faith is not primarily a belief in Christian truth, but a belief in Christ. All truth which we believe, we believe in and because of Him. We know that though we have truly taken Him for our Master, He is very far yet from having told us all that He has to tell. That knowledge does not decrease our satisfaction in believing Him; it increases it; for it binds us to Him not merely by what He has already taught us, but by the far greater truth which He is keeping for us, which He will give us in His good time, and which it is a pleasure to wait for now, as it will be a pleasure to take it when the time shall come. Now, let a believer have this consciousness about his faith; and then, as he stands all radiantly exultant or peacefully blessed in the truth he holds, let the unbeliever come up to him, to pluck away his joy. The well-worn taunt is brought out to be used once more: "How poor your knowledge is! Answer me this, and this, and this, and this. What pleasure can a true man find in such a vague, limited, unscientific faith as yours?" And then the tormentor stands and looks to see the faithful face grow pale, and the light die out of the believing eye. "Now certainly I have taken his joy from him," he thinks. Why is he disappointed? Why should he not be, when what his sceptical brother has been saying to the believer is only what the believer has all along been saying to himself? His favourite word for years has been, "Now I know in part. Only then shall I know as I am known." "We know not yet what we shall be. We only know that when He shall appear we shall be like Him." So he has always told to himself and others the story of his faith and hope. A knowledge consciously imperfect held in the embrace of a perfect nature perfectly trusted—that has always been the condition of his life which he has recognised, which he has loved to state. Why, then, should he be surprised or lose his peace and satisfaction when another hand points out to him what he has known and gloried in so long? The happiness does not fade out of his face. In the embrace and containment of his faith in Christianity within his faith in Christ he has a joy which no man taketh from him.

Always it is the surrounding of the doctrinal faith by the personal faith that keeps the joy of the doctrinal faith safe from attack or theft. You may prove to me that this or that doctrine which I have held for true is not true, you may show me that my creed as a whole is very far from perfect,—my faith, my religion is not lost by such discoveries any more than my love for my friend, which is the delight and inspiration of my life, is turned to hate or indifference when I come to see that there are rooms in his house or regions in his character which I never have entered, or whose furnishings I have misunderstood or misremembered. Of knowledge and faith it is supremely true, as Jesus promised, that when He comes to a thinker and believer, that thinker's and believer's joy is full, and it is a joy which no man can take away from him.

I have but a few moments left to follow our subject—Christ's promise—into one more region, the region of character, the central, inmost region of all life. Can a man have such joy in his own character, in being the thing he is, that no other man can take his joy away from him? Just as soon as we ask ourselves that question, how our imperfections and sins start up before us!

When have I ever stood so pure and clear and irreproachable, with such a blameless front, that the least child, lifting his baby finger and pointing at me as I stood, could not stir my sluggish conscience and make my soul ashamed? What idlest chatterer cannot pluck away our self-satisfaction, and steal the last trace of joy in our own characters? And yet, with all this true, it is not all the truth. There are two different conceptions of character, one of which looks at it in itself; the other looks at it as it is involved with the powers which are at work upon it to make it what it is capable of being. To the first conception, any given character may seem contemptible and mean; to the other, the same character may seem beautiful and glorious. A block of marble or wood lying alone upon a hill-top may be ugly and uninteresting. The same block of wood or marble brought into a sculptor's workshop, though his hands may not have touched it yet, or may have only rudely blocked out his design, may be a thing to reverence, may stir our imagination and our love. And if we may go farther, and attribute to the stone or marble block a thought about itself, a conception of its own value, can we not think that as it lies upon the hill-top it may be ready to accept everybody's disesteem, to believe what everybody says about its worthlessness; but when it comes into the sculptor's hands, it may gain such new sense of its capacity under that wise and loving power that no man's sneer can cloud the pleasure that it feels in the new revelation and hope of its true self which, under those hands, have come to it? Now read the parable. I am a poor, weak, wicked man; I know it; I do not need that you should tell me of it; but when you do tell me, I bow my head and know that you are right. Any small joy in myself which I have been able to conceive, your well-deserved scorn can steal from me in an instant. But now suppose that Christ takes me into His hands. He chooses me. With that indubitable certainty with which the soul accepts His will, I know that He has chosen me that He may make out of me what He sees that I may be. I am a poor dull block still, but I am His. Here in His workshop, here in His church I lie, and His great hands have just begun to shape His purpose in me. I can feel it there, as the dull stone feels the first blocking of the statue. Is not the whole thing changed? Now there is a joy in character which is not present consciousness but certain prophecy, which is not self-conceit but trust in the creative hands whose power I feel upon me. Now there is joy as deep in me as is the yet unwrought design of the dear Lord to whom my soul is given. Now the happiness of the heaven, wherein alone the full result of His great work in me shall appear, is present already in the power of His love. Now let the shrewd critic come and find his fault with me ; now let him point out all the stains and flaws which his keen eyes can see. I am not scornful of his criticism. I welcome it, for it will help me. But it no longer makes me wretched. I am in Christ. Oh, the great meaning of these words! In hope of what He shall make of me, of what He is making of me, my joy abides. It is His intention, not my present condition, upon which I rest, and so I am not wretched. So men cannot steal my joy from me, because they cannot separate me from Christ. So He fulfils His promise : "I will see you, and your joy shall be full, and your joy no man taketh from you."

In one word, then, here lies the limit of the power of our brethren over our lives. All that comes from ourselves, and has its home in our circumstances, they may easily invade. All that comes from Christ, and is in His purpose for our characters, they cannot touch.

This was the safety of the joy of Jesus. It all came from God, and so no maliciousness or carelessness of men could spoil it.

Oh, my dear friends, it is very easy to let men

take from us all that they can take, if only we have in us that of which it is utterly beyond their power to rob us. Let them take our time, our comfort, our peace, even our good name, if only we keep our trust in Christ, and our certainty of everlasting growth in holiness by Him. That no man can take away, because God gave it to us in His Son. That may He give in great assurance to us all.

THE END.

www.ingramcontent.com/pod-product-compliance
Lightning Source LLC
Chambersburg PA
CBHW022023240426
43667CB00042B/1062